LINEAGE SPEAKS

WOMEN WHO CARRY THE TORCH FOR FUTURE GENERATIONS

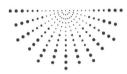

BRIDGET AILEEN SICSKO   ALYSEMARIE GALLAGHER WARREN

ANA MUNOZ   ANDREA BLINDT   ANNELISA VALLERY

ASHLEY ABRAMSON   BRANDY KNIGHT   CHANTEL PORTER

HEATHER ROBINSON   LINDSAY RAE D'OTTAVIO

LYNDSEY HARPER   MARDALENA DAWN TURPEL

MARITÈ SALATIELLO   MELISSA LAMBOUR   MELISSA RUIZ

MIAUWLING OEI   TRICIA MCKENNA   ULRIKE ZIMMERMANN

EXALTED PUBLISHING HOUSE

Dedicated to family, friends, ancestors and loved ones who have come before us. Thank you to all those who will come after us. We love you.

DISCLAIMER

The publisher takes no legal responsibility for the details inside the stories of this book. The words and opinions are the writer's own, the memories they describe are their lived experience and I do not have any evidence that those stories are untrue. I've chosen to trust the authors and have not done them the disservice of fact-checking every version of events. Memoirs are stories from one person's vantage point and these experiences are unfortunately, universal and this is why we've chosen to share them in this collection.

Although the publisher and the authors have made every effort to ensure that the information in this book was correct at press time and while this publication is designed to provide accurate information in regard to the subject matter covered, the publisher and the authors assume no responsibility for errors, inaccuracies, omissions, or any other consistencies herein and hereby disclaim any liability to any party for any loss, damage, or disruption caused by errors or omissions, whether such errors or omissions results from negligence, accident, or any other cause.

Content Warning: This book contains information, stories and experiences that a reader may find disturbing/ traumatic in nature.

CONTENTS

INTRODUCTION

Types a few words...erase, erase, erase.

Again.

Again.

Again.

For days, weeks and over two months, I tried to put words to this book.

How do I introduce it?

How can I put words to the emotions felt here?

What is lineage really?

If you had asked me that question months ago, I personally would've talked about my Irish heritage or coming from a family of women healers, but now I see it as so much more.

Lineage is beyond words. Most of its understanding is actually in the unspoken. The rituals, traditions, beliefs, systems, emotions and language we have accepted for centuries without question. These agreements, as Don Miguel Ruiz would call them, that have permeated our lives without knowing.

But the women whose stories follow these pages began to ask some questions.

Is there another way?

Is there more than meets the eye?

Do I have to hold the same shame those who have come before me have felt or can I release that?

What do I want to pass down to others?

Is it possible to carry the wisdom without the pain?

This book invited me to spaces within myself that I didn't know existed. To hidden places where emotions lay buried waiting for the day when I felt brave enough to meet them with love and compassion. This book invites us all to do just that.

And ultimately, this book provided the healing I didn't know I needed.

Grab your favorite warm beverage, maybe some tissues and buckle up for a beautiful adventure into the depths of who you truly are.

Bridget Aileen Sicsko

ALYSEMARIE GALLAGHER WARREN

UNLEARNING THE UNSPOKEN

*L*et me take the time to open this beautiful space and say this from Mary Magdalene:

> To all the
> words unspoken
> time unbroken
> vows untaken
> lessons undone
> beauty untamed
> pain unleashed
> hearts untied
> doors unopened
> future undecided
> memories unlocked
> lives unhindered
> love unmended.

Because you are here reading our words, I want to thank you. I want to thank you for choosing this path, this place, these pages, this story, this now, this lifetime. Thank you for being open to receive what I am here to deliver. Thank you for honoring the pathways, the portals, the trials, and the hurdles that brought you here.

It's an honor to bring you what's about to unfold. It's an honor to hold space for healing all that has come before now, to create a safe space, to honor the work and the journey that brought you here.

I'm never really sure what's about to be undone when the space of healing opens, when the doors part and healing light streams in, but I'm never afraid to go forward and see what's on the other side—and I invite you to do the same. Close your eyes, take a deep breath, breathe again, and sink into your chair letting this space invite you in. Let the words be spoken, the illusion of time be broken, the vows, the lessons, the beauty, and the pain be undone and unleashed. Let your heart and your door stay open for as long as these pages are in front of you. The future isn't here yet, so no decisions need to be made. All the memories are free and ready to be lived, to be let go, to be healed...right here, right now. All the love knows no limit, no end, no boundaries – this space is all yours for all eternity. The door has been opened and the space will be held for as long as these words live on, for as long as these pages exist. So just sit back, allow, and remember to breathe. You are safe.

When I think about this lifetime, my purpose, and about all I have to say, I start with the things that I first need to unlearn, un-remember, un-know. It is in these moments that I can strip away the masks and see myself as I want to be seen, not as the world wants me to be.

. . .

Let's go deeper than that. Let's go back to before you were you. Let's journey to before your mom knew of you, to before your mom was her, and even before your family began. Let's go to another time in your soul, to the time where we started to learn and understand all that was yet to be known. It is in these moments where lineage began and stories started: this is the beginning of connection. It is in these connections where healing has to happen.

Our problems didn't start in this time or in this place. It did not start with your mom or your grandma or even her mom. Our problems started when we realized we could think, we could feel, we could communicate, and we could form different opinions. But, let me pause and tell you why I'm laying it out like this. I'm saying it like this to remind you that you're not alone, you're not the only one, you're not broken, you're not disconnected. I want you to know that your being here is essential to human connection, to the human timeline, to the passage of time. Each connection we heal is a life that is changed, a life that is saved, a story that is shifted, and a vow that is broken. This is how we heal the stories we pass on.

We've all heard the "I walked uphill both ways to school" stories. We've all been told how easy our lives are now—how different things are now—and with that comes an unspoken burden that we are forced to carry. Unfortunately, we haven't realized yet that making the next generation's load a little lighter is part of our legacy, part of our lineage, part of our story. Why do we shame those who come after us for having an easier life? We should celebrate our work and our successes. Healing is what we are here to do. We are here to undo and unbind the lessons that have been passed on to us generationally.

We are the teachers, the change-makers, the healers, the story tellers, the rule breakers, the success stories that have come to shift the sands of time and rewrite the misguided truths of those that came before us.

If you are anything like me, there are so many things that your family has passed down that were never questioned, never challenged, never even talked about.

"Why do you do it like that?" you ask.

"Because that's just how it's always been done," they reply.

We are taught and trained and expected to follow the rules just as they are written, with an understanding that, because they came before us, they know better.

So, let me ask you to think about one thing you learned from your family that you do, that you've never questioned, never examined, never changed simply because that's how it's always been done. It can be as simple as cutting the ends off roast or whether you decorate your tree on Christmas Eve, or as complicated as how you name your children. Not everything is harmful or needs to be broken, but everything deserves to be questioned... to be thought about...to be examined...to be chosen. Blindly following the leader doesn't always set you up for success and it doesn't allow those who follow after you to have a choice in what comes next.

When you think of your thing, did it come easily? Did it feel heavy or light? Did it feel good? Did it feel like home? What color is it?

Does it want to shift? Does it have a name? Does it feel connected to someone? Does it have a message? Can you see its pathway? Can you see its roots? Is this for me?

This is where I am in my healing of family ties. I'm in the space where healing doesn't need to be messy or hard. Sometimes healing needs just a moment of your time and so many things can be cleared by asking questions.

For me, my family moment was the saying "You have to." This phrase felt like a binding contract that was passed down for ages from woman to woman in my family. This phrase resonated in my bones and felt like a promise couldn't be broken without a mountain of shame.

When I heard this phrase, when I really felt it, I knew in the very core of my being that this is where I needed to explore. This is where I could truly start my unlearning, to release myself and all that came with me, before me, and after me. These were my words unspoken. This phrase resonated so deeply within me that it felt like chains rattling and the whispers of ancestors rejoicing as I broke the links and freed myself—and all of us—from anything we had to do.

This is the beginning, the door opening, the understanding of what had to be done, my "Aha" moment about what comes next. This simple broken contract was the spark that lit a fire within my soul to break everything that bound me but no longer served me. In this moment, I had a true understanding that not every burden I carried was mine to carry.

This may seem like a difficult concept, that not all the burden you carry is yours, but it is important. When it's not our burden to carry, it can be hard to understand how to let it go, how to release it, or even how to recognize it. This is where we have to trust our heart, our gut, and our soul to guide us, the very things we've been taught to question.

So, take a breath, hold your hands up facing each other, close your eyes, breathe again, and feel into the energy created between your hands. Feel the pull of energy. Now breathe into it and sit with it for a moment, take all the time that you need...and when you're ready, put one hand on your heart and the other over your belly button and feel the figure eight, the dance of energy between your hands. This is you, this is your life force, this is the abundance you've come here to have. This is your energy. Breathe into this space. When you feel this and accept this power, you truly feel the call of who you are. This is where the trust begins and you can take the leap to know yourself and un-know anything you've been taught that isn't serving your force. When you ask, it whispers back with a deep knowing of the answer you've been searching for and anything that doesn't resonate with that energy gets to be broken.

You can think about it like cleaning out your closet. You don't have to keep anything that doesn't fit, that you don't wear, that isn't your style, or anything that is out of season. It can really be that easy. Just ask, "Does this serve me? Is this mine? Does this bring me joy?" in whatever words feel good.

The lines of lineage are not linear, are not always clear, and do not follow any rules; and that's where things get messy. You are the only you, and that, my friend, is the only person you are here to serve. We come here to support many people, but only to serve ourselves.

Are you like me? Did you just have a big reaction to the idea that you came here to serve yourself and no one else? Because I did. I thought about all the times I was told that I was here to serve God. And as I sat with this idea, I heard Mary Magdalene urging me forward to a deeper understanding of that message. Somehow, I understood that I was never designed to serve God. God meant for us to bring teachings, to be the teacher, to share God's love, to deepen our knowing and our understanding of truth. We didn't come here to serve but to be of service, and most importantly, we came here to truly live.

This is where breaking the bindings of our lineage really shines, in LIVING. We can't truly be present and serve this lifetime–this *you*–if we're bound and tied to past lives, to ancestors, to past relationships, to old stories. And we are meant to live, fully and completely.

Are you ready yet? On the edge of your seat and ready to take the plunge into cutting ties, breaking chains, unlearning lessons, shifting old stories? No? It's OK, just breathe. Be here right now, tap into your energy and take all the time that you need.

The best thing you can know in this moment is that time is irrelevant, and whenever you're ready is the right time. It's never too late and you're not late. No matter how long you've been putting it off, it's all OK. Keep listening, keep honoring. Keep tapping into your energy and living the best that you can in the moment you have, because that's all any of us can really do.

No need to compare or judge. Live and love yourself fully because you are worthy and deserving of time and space, to show up when you feel ready (or before you're ready!). This is your life to live, so do just that. You're doing everything the way that it is meant to be.

There are no should's, no have-to's, no right way, no better way, no wrong way. Do you hear me? Do you believe me? Can you accept and honor that for yourself? That's what is being asked of you in this moment.

Honor your journey. Honor yourself. Love yourself. Be grateful that you have found yourself here reading these words, holding this space for yourself and for all that will come after you, and for all that has come before you. This is exactly where you are meant to be: honoring your time and space in this moment and allowing your energy to guide you into your next space, your next move on the journey of self-service and living.

Let's close this out by breathing together. Hand over heart, feeling the connection, the lineage of our lives. Feeling our energy, our power, and the collective. Feeling the timelessness of all the ties that bind and all the ties that have been broken–or will be broken–in this life.

Just breathe.

Just be.

You are loved.

You are safe.

You are magic.

You are infinite energy.

You are home.

Every story that you know doesn't serve you is ready to be rewritten.

Every tie that binds you to a place you no longer wish to be tied to is ready to be broken.

Every word that is ready to be spoken, speak it.

Every vow that was contracted is complete and ready to be banished.

Every door that was locked, you hold the key.

When everything feels like it's failing, you put your hand over your heart and breathe.

You are ready and complete.

ABOUT THE AUTHOR

ALYSEMARIE GALLAGHER WARREN

AlyseMarie Gallagher Warren is a Master healer, a healer for healers, and a guide. AlyseMarie has a unique method for awakening one's spirit to their truth as she leads them deeper into their remembering. In the process of healing, she is able to help individuals tap into their own inner voices, inner parts, and highest versions of themselves by guiding them to connect deeper within to their wholeness. AlyseMarie's gifts are deeply rooted in divine love and her connection to Mary Magdalene and Mother Gaia, allowing them to come to her clients in a nurturing, loving, deeply grounded way. AlyseMarie uses the quantum space, guided meditations, painting, Reiki, crystal healing boards, oracle or tarot cards, sound healing, or whatever comes through as the best method for each client. AlyseMarie is an Executive Chef in Chicago and lives in a cute eclectic bungalow with her artist husband, Spence, and their two cats, Kramer and Molly.

www.instagram.com/i.am.alysemarie/

www.linktr.ee/channeledpathways

2

ANA MUNOZ

I REMEMBER

I can remember the day that I found out doulas existed. I was working as a massage therapist at a spa and started a conversation with the woman who would one day be my own birth doula, Nina. It came up in a casual, routine, getting-to-know-your-coworker's conversation: "Do you work anywhere else?" She responded in her sweet Brazilian accent that she was a birth doula. Obviously, the only follow-up to that is, what's a birth doula? Followed by, so you're like a midwife?

You see, a birth doula supports expecting parents throughout pregnancy, labor and birth. They help parents prepare through educational resources, emotional and physical support. Birth doulas help their clients navigate the birthing world and unpack the essence of what their individual ideal birth is. What birth doulas do *not* do is provide the actual medical interventions or procedures. Birth doulas are advocates in helping you choose which procedures you wish to have, but not the providers of the procedures. That is where the medical provider comes in, be it the midwife or the obstetrician.

As Nina explained all of this, my soul was vibrating with excitement as if it were being reunited with a long-lost calling. At the same time, my youth was whispering, "Not yet, young Padawan." The art of being a birth doula is surrendering to the unknown. What day will my client give birth? I don't know. What time will I join them? I don't know. How long will I be there for? I don't know. How will the birth be? I don't know. What will my client need? I don't know, but I'll know when I see them. Every single birth a birth doula commits to is an agreement to the unknown and putting it above whatever else may be going on in their life. I was not yet at that level of selflessness, when I first found out doulas existed at twenty-four years old.

I can remember the day I attended my first birth, three years later. I awoke to my sister's phone call; her water had broken and her provider recommended she head into the hospital to confirm it. I joined her a few hours later and she was surrounded by family as she experienced her contractions come and go. She would sway side to side on the birthing ball, walk around the labor and delivery ward, and experience her labor progress closer and closer to the moment she would meet her baby boy. When the nurse exclaimed my sister could push and everyone had to clear the room, my mother was the first out of the room.

I followed her into the hallway as she cried in anguish. I remember asking my mother why she was crying out of anguish rather than joy. She responded that I had no clue what my sister would soon be experiencing. She was right. In the hours that followed that interaction I watched my sister push on the bed, on the toilet, and back to the bed. I watched as she faced the uncertainty of giving birth and all of the strength that it calls for. I watched as a mother was born, and I was in awe.

I can remember the day three months later when I began my training towards becoming a birth doula. The voice that once whispered to me, "Not yet, Padawan" now spoke, "It's time." I was trained in the stages of birth, what to expect, what the physical, mental and emotional cues were in every stage of labor, how to comfort a mother in labor, how to support the birth partner, how to navigate birth in any setting, be it hospital, birthing center, or at home, and on and on. I was inspired by birth and all it entailed. It was magical, and it was real.

I was also trained in how to prepare the dad to be the advocate. To differentiate the role of an advocate and a birth doula, and that I was the latter not the former. As a birth doula, serving clients in a state that had a higher cesarean rate than the country of Mexico, I was told it was the dad's job to know the birth plan to a T so he could advocate for his partner. My role was to hold space for them and be their walking encyclopedia.

I can remember the day I decided to stop being a birth doula. I was three months postpartum, and I had finally understood why my mom cried the day my sister gave birth to my nephew. I had an amazing labor experience, until I didn't. I remember waking up to the first contraction, the one that made me think, "Oh that was different". Spending the day with my husband in our own little bubble and secret: our daughter was joining us earthside very soon. Being amazed as every surge became stronger, and longer, and yet it was never more than I could handle. Every wave was a reminder of my inner strength. A reconnection to a secret that my body was sharing: I am strong. I am powerful. I am intense. I am connected. I remember the full moon that night, as my doula, Nina, joined us. The hot water from the shower soothing my laboring body, as I swayed and thought of all the mothers out there looking at the same full moon, feeling the same excitement, a feeling of completion bursting in our chest that soon we will meet the little individual who has been present all along, kicking, swimming, and reminding me how amazing this world still is.

I cannot remember in what order things happened when the sun came up. Everything existed at once. Was I in the tub? Was I in the bathroom? When did I get on the toilet? When did I last eat? When did I start pushing? When did I get in the bed? What positions did I push in? Who was in the room? Who was speaking to me? This was Laborland. I had read of it and had seen variations of it with clients. However, experiencing it for myself was an out of this world phenomenon. When you are in it, you don't realize you are in it, and when you realize you are in it, you are no longer in it. It was a paradox. You can only be in Laborland when you aren't thinking about it.

I remember when I left Laborland the first time. I had been pushing, but baby was not budging. I'd give it my all with each push, and sweet baby seemed to be stuck in the same spot no matter how hard I pushed. There were whispers of leaving the comfort of my home and transferring to the hospital beforehand. I left Laborland when I made the decision to head to the hospital. I rose from my bed, was helped to get dressed and out the door we went. It was matter of fact, peaceful, and calm. My baby was well, I was well, and we were just being precautious. I remember the drive to the hospital as I became a back-seat driver, as the midwife continued to monitor baby and me the whole way. I wonder what she thought of my backseat driving. I was definitely far from Labor Land. I was on Route 80 in New Jersey!

I cannot remember how I got back into Laborland. Was it the moment I stepped out of the car? Was it when I stepped past security and walked towards the Labor and Delivery ward? Was it when I walked into my birthing room? How did I get on the toilet? How did I get on the bed? Oh, look, my birth team is back together, plus a nurse now.

I can remember the moment my birth was hijacked. A fiery red, freight train crashed into Laborland, and tore me out of it. After thirty hours of labor, this was the first time I felt pain. I felt anger, I felt rage. And my doula brain turned on. She told me the freight train had the word Pitocin written on the side, and the train was on autopilot so long as she was in my blood. My baby was the thing that had to get out of my body to end this hijacking. So, I pushed in rage. This is why my mom cried that day in December.

Three months later, that rage still lived in me. She was right beside me in the shadows. Silent when all was calm, but one sound from anyone and she was ready to be unleashed. I quit being a doula because of her. I could not hold space for any birthing parents while she was around, uncontrolled and looming, ready to pounce. I was ready to walk away from my calling, give up my dream of holding space to protect my clients from this rage. And yet, walking away was not protecting anyone from her. I saw moms who also knew her, and hid in silence. Our silence was protecting this rage.

I remember when I faced my rage. I cried, I screamed, I punched the bed. I handed my baby to my husband and left the room. I broke a television remote control, I broke the lid of the diaper cream, I broke down. Why did I have to leave my home? Why did I have to transfer to the hospital? Why did I say yes to the Pitocin? Why did my contractions slow down? Why did I feel like I let myself down? Why did I feel like my team let me down? Why did my amazing birth experience have such a nasty ending? How could I hold space for parents experiencing childbirth when I felt so jaded by the experience?

I remember returning to births after facing my rage. My rage was now my greatest tool. She is a guide, right alongside my passion, my love, and my joy for birth. Now, I doula differently, and it is ever evolving. I threw out some of the training that hadn't evolved with the current state of birth. Long gone are the days of telling parents only they can advocate and speak for themselves in their birth space. I am more than a doula. I am an advocate, an educator, a shoulder to cry on, a friend. I was once told that doulas shouldn't share their own birth experience as it is the client's birth we are preparing for, but I now share my birth experience all the time. There are lessons in each birth. Babies are born, mothers are born, fathers are born, and endless possibilities are born.

ABOUT THE AUTHOR

ANA MUNOZ

Ana Munoz is the founder of Morris Prenatal Massage. She is a Massage Therapist and Birth Doula. She believes that more is caught than taught and brings that philosophy into every service she offers to expecting parents. Ana helps expecting parents prepare for birth and transition into their new roles as parents with confidence and support. Ana also hosts a podcast called "Parent By Design" where she shares her knowledge of pregnancy, birth, parenting, and mindset work. She lives in New Jersey with her husband and child.

linktr.ee/morrisprenatalmassage
www.instagram.com/theanamunoz/

3

ANDREA BLINDT

THE POWER WITHIN

Beliefs are passed from one generation to the next, etching deeply into the DNA strands that make us unique. They are taught and modeled so that they are fully integrated in our lives. But what if those beliefs keep you sick? Keep you weak? And keep you powerless? What if those stories ingrained in your genetic make-up are causing you to live small? You get to decide whether or not to keep them, to toss out what no longer serves you, and to rewrite beliefs that allow you to live the life you were created to live.

If Florence Chadwick, a long-distance swimmer, had been told repeatedly that she would never make it, that her vision was too poor to see the island through the fog-lined horizon, her arms too weak, and her desire to accomplish her dreams too small, she would have never become the first woman to swim the Catalina Channel.

Initially, after hours of swimming, Chadwick's mind and body became exhausted. The thick fog surrounding her prevented her from seeing anything beyond her tired moving arms. Riddled by fatigue and unsure of the remaining distance, she started to believe the shore was too far away. That one belief planted in her mind became the anchor that prevented her from moving forward towards her goal, and she requested to be removed from the water. Cocooned in the safety of the boat, she was able to clear her thoughts and absorb her surroundings. She allowed her gaze to locate the distance between where she sat safely in the boat and the shoreline. It was only then that she realized the shore was merely a mile away.

A few months later, utilizing one of the strongest tools she had, Chadwick held a mental image of the shoreline in her mind as she attempted the swim again. Through fatigue and the repeat occurrence of dense fog, she centered her knowing on her ability to reach the shore. She didn't hand her power over to the fear or doubt that crept into her mind, or the perceived failures of her past. Instead, she chose to imagine the outcome she desired and held onto that image until she accomplished her dream. The journey looked different than she had originally envisioned, but it reminded her of the determination, strength, and willpower that lived within her.

In a similar fashion, if I had decided to only listen to the wisdom and guidance of medical providers, if I had chosen to accept their beliefs as reality, my life would be vastly different than it is today. I was taught to listen and put my trust in the adults who had authority, including my parents, teachers, doctors and the government. I believed it was my duty to obey and work daily in order to gain the worthiness and acceptance they offered for being a good compliant follower. I obeyed and relinquished my power to them, acknowledging that they were wiser than I was despite my own medical training and that they had my best interest at heart. Growing up, I was never told that I could have thoughts of my own or a voice that was worthy of being heard. Looking back, perhaps this unknowing stemmed from the lineage I was birthed into as a woman, and the repressions women faced centuries before me: a world and reality where women, much like children, were expected to be seen and not heard. A society where concerns are dismissed and realities twisted to fit the narrative they needed you to believe in order to gain control over you and keep you living out of fear.

Those medical professionals I spent my life looking up to, respectfully admiring and working alongside, painted my future with fear. They created a reality of sickness and dependence on them for medical intervention and support. They convinced me that my dreams were impossible to achieve and that there was no way I would ever have the healing I longed for. They removed the belief of my ability to create life and instead implanted seeds of fear and doubt in my mind.

I endured nineteen surgeries, lost two children five days after they were born, and received multiple autoimmune diagnoses before deciding I'd had enough. My life was full of physical and emotional suffering, and my future looked painfully the same, until I realized I could heal myself by focusing inside my mind.

AUGUST 2019

Screams echoed off the bleak grey hospital walls as I shuffled desperately to soothe him. His body was sticky, feverish from the pain and stress of enduring a six-hour long intensive medical procedure that was going to give us a game plan on how to support his failing body. It had taken two years to get to this point, but we were out of answers and this was our last hope. I swayed, rocking his tiny body back and forth while gently blocking his hands as they clawed at the tubes and wires that lined his intestines and exited his body through a hole in his small distended abdomen. Our son had lived his entire life in constant pain, his abdomen tight from the swelling of his intestines and his mouth full of thick undigested food as it propelled its way from his unmoving stomach through his throat and out of his body. For years, doctors told us this was "normal", that he had "indigestion", that "children threw up", but I knew in my momma heart that this was not normal, that his throwing up was constant and that it was different than my other children's. I knew in my gut, but my voice was repeatedly silenced and our son left each doctor's visit with more medications and dietary restrictions to help manage his never-ending symptoms.

"We were able to see through these tests that your son has a rare disorder. There is no cure currently. Parents usually admit these children and they are placed on enteral nutrition until they eventually fade away." I couldn't comprehend what I had just heard. I blinked slowly, opening my eyes and focusing on the tall doctor standing before me, the flashing light from the computer monitors dancing across his white lab coat grounding me here in this moment. His mouth opened again and he repeated the words, *"No cure, admit him for end of life care..."* Every sound evaporated from the room as the doctor went on to describe the progression of this disease and the symptoms that would ultimately follow. I shut my eyes momentarily and felt my body waver ever so slightly as though it might crumble into a bed of rubble on the hospital floor. I inhaled deeply, filling my lungs with a strength that I knew was not my own. I thanked the

doctor for his time as I worked to gather the various comfort items I had managed to stuff into our diaper bag in an attempt to distract our son during the procedure. Feeling stronger, I turned towards the door just as the doctor informed me that we would have a team meeting in two weeks to set things into place and ensure his entire medical team was up to date on this new diagnosis. I paused at the door, feeling a new peace and knowing fill my body, and then I bravely opened my mouth and let the doctor know that we would *not* be admitting our son, that he would *not* be "fading away" and that I was going to find a way for him to survive. He smirked at me as I reached the door and walked away leaving him and his poor prognosis behind us.

As I reached the car, I could feel my body shaking. I was nervous about what our reality might look like if I couldn't find a solution to help my son live. I was afraid to survive the loss of another one of my children and my heart ached at the thought of not watching him grow up and experience a full life. I had seen many miracles personally and professionally in my medical practice but this was big, this was rare and said to be limiting. I secured my still crying son into his car seat and sat down placing my head gently into the palms of my hands. I closed my eyes and prayed for strength, wisdom, and peace as I went home to update my husband. I didn't know the details but I knew I wasn't going to give up or accept the outcome the doctors had decided upon for our son. I knew that anything was possible, and that if I could find the courage to believe it, I would be able to achieve anything I envisioned.

Immediately, before my husband had a moment to digest the initial shock and devastation of our son's diagnosis, I had decided that we were going to change everything we had been doing medically for him, starting first with the words we allowed to be spoken around him that surely shaped the way he experienced life. I realized that he left each specialist visit sobbing, his pain and nausea amplified, and he appeared more restless and lifeless. I watched my perfect son cry on the floor, gripping his blanket unable to get up, "failing to thrive"—the same label his medical team had given him was the life he was enduring daily. I refused to perpetuate that reality for him and decided to only allow words that created life and hope to exist in his environment moving forward. We wouldn't be speaking about his disorder, his pain or his terminal diagnosis in front of him anymore. We would begin immediately living like he was thriving not like he was dying. We would stop force-feeding him and instead we would provide him with nutritious foods that we knew to be best for him, not the strict diet and medication protocols he had been suffering on for years. We would finally honor him and his body as the absolute masterpiece that it is and we would praise it for every single victory it made, even the teeny tiny ones. We would remind him daily that his body was strong, healthy, and brilliantly created with a mighty purpose. I would stop giving my power away to others, and I would start trusting in my own ability to discern and heal, both myself and my family. I knew creating a change of this magnitude would require conscious effort and the ability to acknowledge and modify the thoughts that played in my mind so that I could express them in a more constructive way. This opportunity for inner growth and empowerment had the potential to create a new way of life that I would be able to share with my children and their children for generations to come.

I spent time deep in thought acknowledging the stories that had survived in my mind for decades, passed into my mind through my ancestors, unknowingly shaping my reality and the ways I perceived life. Beliefs and limiting thoughts were the unwanted gifts that I had received as a young child and that day I chose to consciously begin to change them in order to rewrite them. As I sat sorting through the stories and disempowering beliefs, I noticed how as a young child I was trained to respect my elders, taught that doctors were to be idolized, that they had power because they were knowledgeable and that what they said was a fact and should never be questioned. I was directed to show my respect by obeying them and their commands regardless of what my inner knowing knew to be right for me. I realized that by allowing them to influence me and my beliefs, I had prevented myself from honoring my true knowing, and as a result, had been harmed multiple times by the medical practitioners who had taken an oath to do the opposite. I recognized that for a majority of my life I had given my power away to doctors or authority figures and allowed them to dictate my health, my healing, and the outcomes I believed to be possible in my life. And then I realized that I had the opportunity to change that all. I acknowledged that I am my own best advocate, not someone who doesn't know the intricate details that shape the person I am from the inside out.

One of the biggest opportunities we have for personal growth and healing occurs when we as humans or medical providers allow our minds to be open to the possibility of different healing modalities rather than only exploring the ones we already know. Change is often challenging and requires awareness and accountability in order to mindfully expand and evolve, but by becoming conscious we allow our minds to be open to possibilities and solutions that weren't there before. I placed my traditional nursing education on hold and spent weeks researching therapies and treatments I had never heard of while studying western medicine. I joined support groups and became educated on the intricate details of the disorder I knew our son would overcome, from real people who were currently living with the condition despite medical belief that they ever would. I became certified in hypnotherapy and created a custom script for our son that targeted healing, strength, and peace from pain. He listened to his recording multiple times a day, allowing the belief of his body's ability to heal and become the dominant neural pathways in his mind. I studied nutrition, homeopathy, flower essences, and applied kinesiology in order to fully utilize all the tools needed to heal his body fully all the while rejuvenating my own.

Healing my son was one of the most magnificent catalysts that propelled me forward in my business and in the type of services I am able to offer my patients today. I believe we all have the potential to overcome any health challenge when we are given the right information and support. When we choose to partner with providers who inspire, empower, and explore options alongside us instead of independently for us. Through this unique healing method, I realized I had the power to change anything I wanted, and I learned that in order to fully thrive, the changes needed to start from within. I became the architect of my mind and healthcare, and I found the strength to reclaim my power. It was mine, after all. I allowed myself to honor my past and move through the pain to find the gifts and lessons it contained. Today, my voice is stronger because I chose to consciously learn through my struggles. I am educated, empowered, and full of gratitude in every area of my life, even the sticky hard parts, because I know that even those have the potential to bring healing if I allow them to. I expanded my knowledge and found a way to bring harmony into my life and inspiration to each day. Emotional strength was not something I was born with, but I was able to grow it by persevering through the hardships in my life. I found true resilience by changing the old beliefs that played on repeat in my mind and shifting them into more empowering ones that made me feel good instead. This conscious ability to think again for myself serves as a daily guide, and illustration to my children and myself, about the power to manifest the lives we desire. The path towards natural healing wasn't painless, but I understand now, that without the suffering I experienced, I wouldn't be the amazing woman I am today.

The woman I am now is full of grace and compassion, and I'm honored to be her. I am wise, committed, and a fierce advocate for what is right. I'm married to my best friend, a man who is steadfast and full of love. He is my biggest supporter and it's truly a gift to be his wife. Together, we have four beautiful living children, full of life and purpose, each one unique and brilliantly thriving today. By choosing to reclaim my power and rewriting the beliefs in my mind, I was able to cut the cord that kept me attached to the dysfunctional thought patterns of my lineage, and instead used my mind as the powerful tool it is. I created healing and happiness in my life and model that opportunity to my children daily. I'm grateful I chose to live my life this way; believing in myself and my ability to thrive has blessed me in so many ways.

I encourage you to rewrite your story, to release the beliefs and traumas that are preventing you from living the life you crave. Become inspired to create a new way, dream big, and persevere until you find the healing that is yours to claim. You have the power to overcome anything and to live a life that makes you happy and eager to wake up for, one that excites you and allows hope to shine through you into this world. Ups and downs will inevitably come your way, but it is my desire for you that you would find strength along the way, knowing that you have the power within you to go through it all. You are not alone and don't need to be. You are loved, you are worthy, and designed to be free.

As the sufferings in my life threatened to bury me, I learned that there were two ways in which I could respond to the situations in my life: either by succumbing to the weight and darkness of my surroundings, or by persevering through the shadows, becoming my own light. I chose to ignite!

ABOUT THE AUTHOR

ANDREA BLINDT

Andrea Blindt is a registered nurse, inspirational mentor, and founder of Growing Miracles. Over the past twelve years, she has partnered with families around the world to share ancient wisdom for modern medical challenges. Andrea loves helping women grow their families through hormone balance, fertility rejuvenation, and mindful parenting. Andrea leads from a place of deep personal knowingness and resilience that has allowed her to heal herself and her family from multiple disorders. She shares her incredible journey in order to inspire hope in her patients. Andrea creates space for people to be seen, heard, and loved as they reclaim their power and heal from the inside. Andrea has been featured on Natural Health Radio, Conceive IVF, and has spoken at many events. She lives in California with her wonderful husband and four beautiful children. In her free time, she loves to read, write, hike, and spend quality time with her family.

www.rngrowingmiracles.com
www.instagram.com/andreablindt/
www.andreablindt.com

4

ANNELISA VALLERY

GIFTS WRAPPED IN SANDPAPER

"*The wound is the place where the light enters you.*"
~Rumi

When people see me, they see a woman who is pure love, joy and connection. I am an entrepreneur, a career woman, a teacher, and an intuitive energy healer who has a powerful presence in the world serving her community, a fierce work ethic and loves her family dearly. A large part of who I am comes from my maternal grandmother who I affectionately called Granny. Granny's love and devotion to our family's success was unwavering, fierce and pure love. What I know now about Granny is that she loved me unconditionally, she saw the best in me even when I didn't see it in myself and she only wanted the absolute best for me. Nothing less. Granny had a vision of me thriving, and she provided a solid foundation for me when I didn't even know I needed it. She has been a guiding force throughout my life and from the Spirit realm, she continues to be.

But it wasn't always this way. The summer before my ninth birthday, my mom, my little sister and I went to live with Granny and Pappy shortly after my parents divorced. My world was turned upside down; it was ever changing, shifting and morphing right before my eyes. In what felt like the blink of an eye, we left my dad behind in Georgia and moved to New Jersey, where Granny and Pappy lived. At that time, life was moving so fast, I felt like I couldn't catch my breath. Nothing felt like solid ground for me to stand on. I had witnessed one of the last blowout arguments my parents would ever have. It got so intense that it escalated to Mom yelling at me to run to the neighbors to call the police. As quickly as my parents' argument had started, it stopped—just before I grabbed the doorknob of the carport door leading to outside. That moment remains frozen in my memory.

We arrived at Granny's house. It was a place that felt familiar yet it was so foreign. Prior to our move, we had only spent short periods of time with Granny and Pappy, visiting here and there for vacation or the holidays when the entire family was around. At first, it was okay. I was learning the new landscape: new people, new rules, and foreign family dynamics all while navigating the sadness in my heart that my family was no longer the unit I thought it was. In this new world, three generations were under one roof with three distinct sets of rules: Mom's, Granny's, and Pappy's. Of all of them, Granny's rules were the most stringent.

At first, it was good. I discovered that Granny and I both enjoyed music and we loved to sing. Granny was in many choirs and singing ensembles. We would always go to her concerts and performances when they were local. Pappy always recorded them, every single one. What I loved most though, was going with Granny to the rehearsals. I especially loved her rehearsals with the Sweet Adelines, because not only did they sing, they had choreography for some of the songs. It was so much fun. I remember several times when they were performing in the community and I was invited onto the stage to sing with them, because naturally, I knew the song and the moves.

Then, things began to shift. I completed my fourth grade year with As and Bs and all the adults seem to be pleased. My fifth grade year ended with similar results. After some time living with Granny and Pappy, our communication with my dad started to dwindle and the cards for birthdays and holidays stopped coming. The sadness only deepened, but that didn't mean life stopped. Life was still happening all around me. My grades started to slip and life became an empty performance. I got tired of playing pretend. Granny's critiques of my performance and how I was showing up never took a vacation. It was constant. When I mustered up the energy to give my best to an activity or a task, or even managed to pull my grades up, Granny's feedback was the same; she focused on what I didn't do, what looked awful, what was left sloppy, what needed to be redone or simply, what she didn't like. I gave up trying to please her and gave up performing.

I felt alone and disconnected as I navigated my inner journey of sadness and pain. It seemed nothing I did was ever good enough. There was so much focus on my performance in the world: be nice, mind your manners, get good grades, be polite, act ladylike, take neat notes, do your homework, clean your room, help your mom... and the list goes on. My inner world was filled to capacity with so many conflicting emotions, yet there was little to no attention paid to any of it. It appeared to only matter how well I could pretend that all was well and how well I could perform.

Then came my high school graduation. I reluctantly and begrudgingly invited Granny and Pappy because "Mom said I had to." Ugh! Although I had hoped that maybe for one night, we could all celebrate me and it could be good, there was also another part of me that knew it may be more of the same.

Graduation day came and I was so excited. Finally, I finished the shenanigans they called "school" and I could start studying the things that I was actually interested in. At that time, we lived in Pennsylvania and Granny and Pappy had arrived that morning while I was getting ready. I left the house shortly after they arrived with just enough time to say "Hello" and "See you later". I felt like I was skipping to my high school graduation, even though I was driving, excited to complete this milestone .

The music began to play and I walked out with my fellow graduates onto the grass, beaming with pride. When I sat down, I couldn't see my family in the stands. I thought nothing of it and just focused on the ceremony and listening for my name to be called. Graduation ceremony came and went, but when the ceremony was over, I looked around to see everyone else with their family and yet, I couldn't find mine. Who I did find was my dear friend, Steve. We stood for a moment waiting for Mom, my little sister, Granny and Pappy, but after everyone started to clear out, I then decided that we should just meet them at the car. I found the car, and as I excitedly began to ask my mom if I could go and hang out with friends to celebrate tonight, I noticed the look of upset in her face. I didn't let it bother me because I wasn't about to let whatever happened get me down. She asked that we meet them back at the house, so I agreed. When Steve and I arrived back at my house, I heard fussing from outside—mostly Granny's voice. I unlocked the door and began to walk upstairs and all I heard Granny say is, "I am not proud of her. I am not proud of her." This couldn't be happening, not today, of all days. She then went on to list out the reasons she is not proud of me. At first, I wasn't sure who she was talking about. The moment it all sank in that she was referring to me, the tears began to stream down my face. I looked at my mom wanting her to speak up and say something, anything, to reaffirm that I had just completed another milestone in my life. She looked at me and said, "Just go, get changed and you can go with your friends." As I turned to head back to my room to change, Steve was behind me. My 5'3" grandmother then came right in his face and asked, "Are you proud of her?" Steve replied, "Yes, I am very proud of her." Granny didn't skip a beat and replied, "Well, I am not." She continued her rant, as I frantically changed clothes and rushed back to the front room. Mom rushed us out of the house and the moment we sat in Steve's little green Fiat, I broke down in tears. Why was she not proud of me? Did I not just graduate high school? Did I not just complete my first major milestone in my teen life?

From that day forward, I swore I would never go out of my way to please her again. I would be cordial and even that had its limits. The anger I had towards my grandmother for the way she treated me growing up then began to fester and resentment began to grow. What did I ever do to this woman to be treated this way?

I threw myself into all of the jobs that I had at the time - usually at least two. I ensured that when she planned to visit, I planned to work twelve hour days. On holidays, I preferred to be anywhere she wasn't going to be, and if I had to be, I steered clear of being caught in one-on-one conversation with her.

Although college graduation went much better with Granny and Pappy present, I still resented Granny and stuck to my plan to steer clear. In my third year of college, I started to take personal development courses with the encouragement of my aunt, a dear family friend. After college, I began to reflect on my relationship with Granny, how I was treated growing up and the way she compared my performance to that of my younger cousins. As I remembered the moments, when I was left dealing with the impact of her harsh words and comparisons, I also began to notice that as angry as I was with her, for what felt like the first time ever, I began to see the principles and lessons that she had embedded in me. It was like I saw a glimmer of the love she had for me. Now, to be clear, it definitely didn't even compare to the numerous paper cuts my heart moved through growing up with her. Yet, it was the first moment I could acknowledge, growing up with Granny was rough, and she was also one of my greatest teachers. Damn! Honestly, it felt awkward admitting that to myself. How could the same woman who caused me so much grief be one of my greatest teachers? This was the first moment I experienced a glimpse of the light entering through the wound. It felt unfamiliar and weird.

As Granny aged, she developed dementia. At first, it was only the stories she told that got repeated several times in one conversation. Eventually, she began to revert to her five year-old self, which was quite the role reversal adventure. I had worked with dementia patients before, so I was familiar with how the disease progresses. But there was one conversation we had after she had moved into the advanced stages of dementia that left me in awe.

As Granny and Pappy aged, Mom moved in to care for them in their home. Mom wasn't great at answering her cell phone, so when I wanted to speak to her, sometimes I had to call Granny's house phone. This particular day, Mom wasn't answering her cell phone after numerous attempts. So, I called Granny's house phone and to my surprise, Granny picked up the phone. It was going to take mom some time to get to the phone, giving Granny and I a moment to chat. We started with small talk about work, life, and a wealthy young man (you know, the man Granny had a vision of in her mind as my husband). As our chat was coming to a close, she paused. She said, "I love you," and I returned her sentiments thinking that was the end of the conversation. Then, she paused and repeated "I Love You" with greater emphasis as though I hadn't heard her the first time. Maybe I didn't. I remember looking at the phone wondering "Is this MY grandmother?" I remember saying: "Yes Granny, I know you love me. I love you too." It felt as though in that brief moment that she really wanted me to get how much she loved me like I had never heard her before. Finally, mom got to the phone. She and I spoke for several minutes thereafter, but once we completed our call, I stopped whatever multitasking I may have been doing at that time. I replayed that moment I just had with Granny over and over in my mind. Did I just have a loving moment with Granny? Hm. That was odd. This was the second moment where I felt the light enter through an old wound.

Fast forward to November, two months before Granny's 90th birthday. Mom informed me that Granny had been shifted to hospice care for comfort. I was preparing to travel abroad, taking some time for some well-deserved self-care. While I was away, in my introspections, my relationship with Granny came up for me.

The emotionally-charged resentment I still was holding onto bubbled up for me to let go. It was calling to be released from my heart. I sat with a few questions: What if the story I was telling myself was not true? What if Granny were a human being creating life for herself, her family and others in the best way she knew how, demanding excellence at every turn? What if this tireless demand for excellence was training and development for a larger purpose? Would I resent my teacher for the greatest gift she gave me? Could I let go of the hurt I experienced while honoring the gold she gifted me?

The message I received was: When we come into this world, our family is not given an instruction manual, or a how-to guide on the best way to raise us. They use what they know to raise us. The elders see what's missing and although they know what is to be planted, there is no manual or guide to show them how to plant it. So they do the best they can with the knowledge they have to ensure the seeds are planted. Sometimes the scars left feel like thorns, and it is up to us to choose to release the thorns and appreciate the beauty of rose blossoming.

Wilma Francis, aka Granny was an only child whose mother demanded excellence at every turn and taught her the very seeds she planted in me.

- Never say you can't, you can do anything you put your mind to.
- Don't do things just because others are. Think for yourself and make your own choices.
- Don't let others change who you are, do what you know is right always.

- Deliver your best always, even when you think no one is watching or you are just "practicing". Always give your best.
- Take pride in your appearance and everything you do.
- Go for the things you really want.

Through my healing journey, I discovered that all the seeds that Granny had planted contributed to the woman that I am today. Although the tilling of the soil that happened throughout my youth was gruff, the solid foundation she laid created the proper conditions for the seeds she planted to come into full bloom as me.

ABOUT THE AUTHOR

ANNELISA VALLERY

AnneLisa Vallery is a teen/youth advocate, an intuitive activation coach, and the founder and President of Causing Legacy. Through her service as a CASA (Court Appointed Special Advocate) for children and teens in the Los Angeles County foster care system as well as her relationships with her elders and her own healing journey, AnneLisa was inspired to serve BIPOC teens and youth on a larger scale and be a bridge for intergenerational connections. Through Causing Legacy, she facilitates experiences that honors the elders' wisdom and contributes to teens and youth by providing them tools, resources and support to heal, navigate the inner journey, and discover who they are in the world. AnneLisa has also been featured in *The Turning Season* podcast.

www.causinglegacy.org
www.instagram.com/annelisavallery/

5

ASHLEY ABRAMSON

EARTHLY HUGS AND SOUL KISSES

The following pages are a letter to my father, from my perspective, of what our earthly journey looked like, how it had an impact on me and how I was able to turn our messes into my purpose and message. We are continuing on this journey together and leaving a legacy of walking home one person at a time to their authentic self.

---

*D*ad,

I am now thirty-eight. Twenty years have passed since we saw one another last and we are coming up on the twenty-year anniversary of you completing your journey on this earth. I have so much to share with you which I'm sure you already know, but I want to share my experience of this journey we are on together that went from earthly to now soul.

This letter is to share with you how your earthly journey has impacted my earthly journey in so many ways, and how through your journey and mine we are now having an impact on others to find their own happiness within and live unapologetically as their truest selves.

Dad, my earliest memories of you are that of pure happiness, joy, gratitude, love and full fuck-yes fun! Your heart and soul were as pure as a child and you radiated an energy so contagious you could light up a room. There was never a dull moment in your presence. We were constantly experiencing life at its purest form, constantly active, laughing and smiling. You were my favorite person to be around and now I know why, because we had a pure soul connection. Money was never your focus—instead it was just pure enjoyment of life. If you didn't have the money to buy things, you still always found a way.

As I grew older though, I realized the way others looked at you and talked about you. The message I received was that you were not responsible, you were child-like, you were not reliable, you were not worthy and, ultimately, you were just too much for them. I began to take on the views of others and began to be embarrassed by you because you didn't fit in with everyone else. You were never quiet, you were not shy, and you never dimmed your light, so you always stood out in a crowd.

As time went on, I became a part of the adult conversations, hearing that you were mentally unstable and an alcoholic. So, what I had once seen as the most joyful way of being, I realized was actually seen by others as something bad and not acceptable. I realized that in order to live a life where I would be accepted, I needed to dim my light and fit in with the rest of society by creating a life that was shadowed and supported by others, even if not in full alignment with my desires.

Dad, our relationship was more than a father-daughter relationship. You were a soulmate. You understood me and I understood you! We both shared intense energy and a pure love for life and experiencing that is so rare. We both were not easily accepted by others and constantly directed to dim our lights for others. You never did though, you just kept shining bright. I loved spending time with you because I could shine so bright and there was no judgement. Instead, we fed off of one another, shining brighter together. I remember playing video games late one night together (when we were supposed to be sleeping). And when I told you that sometimes I feel like killing myself, and most parents would immediately go into how-do-we-fix-this, you didn't. You met me without any judgment and spoke of how you could relate to feeling that you couldn't be yourself. You assured me that I was worthy of being happy and being the brightest light out there and I believed you. I remember going back home to Mom's on cloud nine because I was going to shine my light so bright and just be me. I was immediately brought back to reality when I went to school that Monday and people were teasing me and asking what was wrong with me because I was being so loud and annoying. So, I again dimmed my light and this experience reiterated the fact that if I wanted to be accepted, I needed to become someone that I was not. I needed to dim my light to be received and accepted by others. Over the years I would attempt to shine my light bright only to have the narrative, that I couldn't be me, validated by others and once again I would shut it down.

I continued to push further away from you, Dad, because you didn't follow that construct and you just continued to shine your light despite everyone around you pushing further away from you. You were hospitalized multiple times for mental health, and anyone who interacted with you treated and talked to you like a child. I remember dreading going to your house because it reminded me of who I was but that I was not allowed to be her anymore.

I began to push the people around me away as well. I moved out of Mom's and lived with a friend's family. One day, I realized that I was so alone and couldn't be myself, so why stay on this earth? What was the purpose? That is when I chose to take my own life and end this journey here on earth. As you know, I was almost successful, and for a moment the medical doctors shared that my journey was ending. Then, my body did something miraculous and pulled me out of a situation that was explained as medically impossible. You didn't visit me during this time though and I never asked you why. I'm guessing it's the same reason why I dreaded visiting you; likely because my situation was a mirror for where you were at, because only eight months later, you were successful in ending your earth journey.

I spent some days in the children's ward after attempting to take my own life where there were children who were dying and didn't want to. It was the most humbling experience ever. That is when I decided my purpose here was larger than me and I dedicated my life and happiness to being a servant for others and ensuring their happiness. I then entered a treatment center where you did come to visit and again I was so embarrassed to have you there. You shared your dreams of buying an RV and traveling around the country, which I thought was irresponsible and not what people "should" do.

This treatment center advised me to cut off communication with you because you were unhealthy for my recovery, so I did. I would ignore your attempts to contact me, and eventually you stopped. During this time, I again would test the waters by shining my light and again was shown that was unacceptable. I actually almost got kicked out of the treatment center because of that. During that time, I was diagnosed with bi-polar just like you. They based their diagnosis on what they termed as me being in a constant state of mania along with the history of your diagnosis. I was placed on very strong mood stabilizers that essentially turned me into a zombie who just didn't feel anymore. This was perfect, because the Ashley who was not to be seen and who was meant to be locked away, was easier to hide. Yes, she did come out at times, although it was very short and it was much easier to dim her light on the medications.

Then months after I left the treatment center, you reached out and I agreed to meet up with you, but you never showed up. I am still not sure why but have a feeling again that I would have been a mirror that you were not willing to face at that time.

That November I had a dream—well, I would say more of a nightmare—that you had taken your life. It was the kind of dream where, when you wake up, you still feel that heaviness knowing it's not real but still feeling that it is. Later that day, I was at work and got the call...Mom called me, and she never calls me at work. She told me she was coming down to visit me but her energy seemed off. I immediately said "It's him isn't it," and she said yes, and that you had taken your life. I fell to my knees and sobbed as the immense guilt, shame and disbelief took over. Though, like I said before Dad, I had a sense of knowing already that this event had occurred, but still, it was devastating. I was eighteen and due to your recent divorce from your second wife, I was your next of kin. I received everything from the sheriff's department including your suicide note in which you shared that you had no one left and no purpose so why should you go on. Those words and the action you took by successfully taking your life changed my life right then and there as well.

I vowed first off to never have children and pass on these horrible genes. Secondly, I vowed that I would officially lock the free, fun-loving, passionate person that I was away forever. I realized in that moment if I continued to toy around with allowing her out that your reality would become my own. I became the most unhappy, uptight individual who was constantly exhausted from being someone she was not. I went on like this for years, doing my best to fit in and not be seen. I met a man and his son who I fell in love with and vowed to take care of them forever. It was my life's mission to build the family that society wanted me to have, or so I thought. I modeled for them to also fly under the radar and fit in with everyone around us, as I subconsciously knew what the outcome was if we did not.

I went to college and got a degree in social work to again dedicate my life to others. With my unsuccessful suicide attempt and your successful suicide attempt, I had created the narrative of who I was meant to be. I was meant to live a life as a servant to others, never to enjoy my own life and to only find happiness through external things and through ensuring everyone around me was happy and safe.

I continued to be on heavy mood stabilizers for years, always having awful side effects and never staying on one for long but the stronger they were the better because now my mission was to never allow my truest self out again. I was filled with anxiety, extreme anger, rage, resentment and a displeasure for life. The only way to find small doses of happiness was through the external gratification of building a life that looked amazing to others, purchasing new items and ensuring that all of the people around me were happy and constantly being taken care of by me.

I had a few different counselors over the years, and one of my counselors said, "I do not believe you have bi-polar." From there, we started going off my medications, which was a rollercoaster to say the least. It was also a struggle because my authentic self would start to come out and she was harder to keep inside. Around that same time, I had secured my first real job, a job dedicating myself to helping others in the world of child protection. Life was great, and I had even found an ability to allow my authentic self to come out every now and then—through drinking. Dad, when I was drinking, my child's love for life was not questioned. Dancing, singing and grinning ear to ear was acceptable because, well, everyone was doing it. I was not becoming this person due to the influence of alcohol, instead I was using alcohol as a mask to allow my authentic self out. Life was perfect. My authentic self had opportunities to let loose and be herself without judgment. I was married, I had my dream home and the cars, and we were what appeared to the world to be the perfect family.

Then shit hit the fan, Dad. In a matter of seconds, my entire infrastructure that I had built and thought I had full control over was ripped out from under me. I was getting a divorce and it was completely out of my control! I fell apart! If I had owned a gun during that time Dad, I wouldn't be living out this journey on earth. I would be with you, wherever that is. So instead, I just did everything in my power to live like I was dead. I would go to the bar every night, get blackout drunk and do things that were unthinkable! I completely self-destructed to the point that I scared myself. I was lost. I had nothing and no one! I lost my son, husband, dog, cats, house, cars and ultimately the control over myself and my own life! That control of the "perfect" life was what I had needed in order to keep my authentic self, who was either a lighthouse or a destructor, at bay. I had nothing and felt like I wasn't worth anything. I cussed God out and vowed to never trust him again. Heck, I cussed you out on multiple occasions because your selfish ass left me in this mess of a world where no one accepted me! This went on for at least a year. I am surprised I wasn't assaulted, ended up in jail, killed or overdosed on what I could get my hands on.

Then came another soulmate. She was a woman at work who was a supervisor, and I despised her pure heart and love for life. I always thought she had rose-colored glasses and wished she could just see reality. Then, due to my increase in calling in sick to work and not doing the paperwork necessary to complete my job, I was placed on an improvement plan at work. They made me meet with this woman. But now, I truly believe she was a light that you sent me, a mirror in which I needed to see myself in order to turn our mess into a message. She was so similar to you but so different. She met me without judgment like you did, and like you, she never tried to fix me. In fact, she encouraged activities that brought out my authentic self who was filled with love and excitement for life! She was the person that helped me find my path back home.

At first it was terrifying. Dad because, well you know, our light is very bright and is often too much for others. When you have spent your entire life trying to dim your light and then you let it out, well, it's even scary to yourself. There were many times that it was so powerful that I would start to look through the lenses of others and think that maybe in fact I am manic, but I maintained this deep knowing that this is who I am.

I continued on this journey for some time, and in the process, I realized that I never wanted another person to feel as alone and filled with shame and guilt like I had after my divorce. So, I started coaching women after divorce, and in that process, I realized that divorce can be one of those earth-shattering life events that becomes an actual blessing and opportunity to find our way back home to our most authentic self.

I continued to uncover and fully step back into my authentic self, realizing how beautiful life actually is when you show up as yourself with only the purpose of soul connection with others. Through this journey, I also was able to see the impact of our relationship and how I had locked my authentic self up due to the lens that society had viewed me through. I was able to rebuild a relationship with my inner child and heal the deep-rooted traumas I had experienced that had brought me to the place of complete hollowness inside. When I finally fully stepped into my authentic self, it was freeing, and I was filled with love and gratitude. Yes, there are people that still struggle to accept my energy, but at the end of the day, I know it is because I am a mirror for them and that their response has nothing to do with me.

I have also healed one of the biggest wounds I was carrying—the shame and guilt tied to your death. I truly believe that our purpose is to awaken others, and though losing you was one of the hardest things I have been through, it was necessary. Our work together was never meant to be solely done on a human level. Instead I believe it was meant to be completed on a soul level, and my human journey is the vessel that is bringing our journeys into full light!

I have since, through much research and organic transformation, become a Mentor for Dynamic Leaders. I have realized that being stuck in the "hustle culture" is one of the most accepted and least discussed addictions we have. What people are trying to cover up and run from is their authentic self. Why? Because it scares them just like it scared me. I have worked through those fears and now enjoy every single day here on this earth. I am able to see the blessings in even the toughest times and it is because I am becoming freer every day! Free from the constructs that society, myself and my family have created for me. I am rewriting my narratives, our narratives. I now am open to the idea of children because I now know what was really going on. Dad, you were just being authentically you, and society did not know how to handle a light so bright. They placed their judgement and labels on you, and caused you to question your own truth, causing confusion and ultimately your death. I'm not saying this is society's fault entirely because, well, as my favorite quote goes, "it's not your fault if you are fucked up, but it sure as hell is your fault if you stay fucked up." Though society and the people around us may have created constructs that we have taken on, that doesn't mean that we can't choose to rewrite those narratives by healing our inner child.

Dad, today I am utilizing my extensive training on childhood trauma, our journey together and my own healing wisdom, to walk with others on their journey back to their authentic selves where they can live a life of happiness and love that comes solely from within!

I have turned our mess into a movement, Dad, and I have named it "The Unicorn Effect Method". I chose the word "Unicorn" because the unicorn is a magical and mythical creature that we've been told we will never see and can only dream of. We may have learned along this journey that our authentic self is meant to be locked away but, as you and I know, when you believe in magic and you embody magic, it is absolutely possible to be fully seen as our magical self.

Dad, I'm leading a life of gratitude and love, walking with others on their path back home to their authentic selves and I know I am not doing this work alone. Your soul now lives on in me!

Love always,

Ashley

ABOUT THE AUTHOR

ASHLEY ABRAMSON

Ashley's life purpose is to guide workaholic, six-figure earners back into alignment, so they can step into their most authentic selves and live a life of bliss and abundance.

After over a decade as a social worker, Ashley found herself chasing someone else's dream. Ashley knew that she was meant for more and took a leap of faith into her most magical life. Her goal is to blend her wisdom and expertise of the impact childhood traumas have on adults. She uses a strengths-based approach to help high-earners find their magically authentic selves.

Ashley guides her clients to discover who they are through inner child work, rewriting narratives that are true to their authentic selves, and integrating daily skills to remain in alignment.

Ashley believes that everyone should learn how to step into alignment and gratitude. Her podcast, *The Unicorn Effect*, encourages ways to do that.

www.instagram.com/ash_abramson/
coachwithashley.net

6

BRANDY KNIGHT

FOR THE CHILDREN

*T*he Golden Chain, according to Kundalini Yoga, is a profound teacher-student bond where both parties are deeply dedicated to the lineage of teachers and the teachings that came before. Ultimately, the student becomes the teacher in passing down the teachings to their students, and thus the Golden Chain continues.

My teacher, Guru Jagat, imprinted a legacy so deep into this time and space that the Golden Chain has created an indestructible web of wisdom across the planet and beyond. Her dedication to her lineage, piercing insight and razor-sharp delivery cut through any Piscean spiritual bypassing wads of bullshit that have plagued the esoteric and new age scene over the years.

It wasn't that Guru Jagat and I were friends, or even that I agreed with her about everything. In truth, we never physically met during this life. Our connection was completely about her fully embodied teaching style. She taught us all who showed up and kept up how to live in a way of being blunt and loving, in your face honest and accountable, self-first and compassionate. It is something unique beyond words that can articulate what this woman taught me through her embodied leadership while I was working with her. Beyond the Yogic teachings, beyond the alchemy transmissions, and even beyond the unparalleled fashion, she taught me by example how to be a straight-up badass. How to be unapologetically Alpha Female.

One of the first things I think about when I hear the word "unapologetic" is accountability. True unapologetic living oftentimes rubs people the wrong way if they are not taking accountability for their lives. For example, I no longer feel the need to apologize for my behaviors because I know I am consciously doing my best. In turn, I no longer require other people to apologize to me for stuff that might hurt or piss me off because I know we came together to learn and grow. I chose this life whether or not I remember doing so. It is a light code that is imprinted into my thirty trillion cells. I take full accountability for calling in every little thing in my life. Whether it was called in consciously or subconsciously, I made that shit. I know now that when shit hits the fan, it is a gift I give myself that lets me know I am ready for an upgrade. I create it all so that I can honor my mission. Fierce accountability and full responsible emotional expression is true strength. Using my voice, my sound, from a place of deep accountability is complete power. Complete Alpha.

I spent so much of this life wrestling with a deep desire to be a fully embodied Alpha. When I was younger, I would shove down my emotions, play dumb, push aside my abilities and gifts. At moments, I fearfully took on toxic beliefs and behaviors from certain lineage traditions. It was as if I was just doing and believing things because that is how it had been done for so long without question. I witnessed at a young age that powerful women often got ridiculed. That they were labeled loud, rude, even evil! I knew deep down though, from a very young age, that I chose a powerful mission in this life that would require my unbridled life force regardless of ridicule. That scared the shit out of me. I was so terrified of my power. I was terrified of my voice, my sound. I was terrified of other people's judgments and opinions. Yet I knew, at some point, I would have to shed those layers like a newborn baby shedding the caul. I knew that I had to get loud and find my voice because I again chose as my mission to be a part of an awakened lineage. A lineage of highly conscious and fiercely embodied teachers. I came here to be a link in the Golden Chain.

I had studied alchemy and esotericism for years before my daughter arrived. Yet it wasn't until I became a mother that I experienced alchemy on some next levels within my system. My daughter and I started communicating telepathically from the moment we first made eye contact. It was my baby girl reflecting my mission to me in those early moments of motherhood that shook me into remembrance. I saw our crystalline coded contract and dedicated myself to honoring it.

Being a mommy helped me uncover all the emotions I had been hoarding, and all those backlogged emotions that had been passed down within my family lineage. I was, and continue to be, completely dedicated to releasing those emotions that have been held on to for so long. Completely committed to healing and growing on every level, for myself and the family lineage. I was now ready to get big, get loud, find my voice, and generate power from my sound. For my daughter and for me, her mother, the mother, the ma.

Sound creates form. Absolutely everything is sound. That sound is vibrational frequency. The denser the sound, the stronger the frequency, the denser the form. Mantra chanting is practiced across the planet and has been since the beginning of time itself. Some of the first passages ever written refer to physical reality being created by words, by mantra, by sound. Law of Attraction teaches us that thoughts manifest things into physical reality. Those thoughts are transmissions we receive in accordance with how we are focused. For example, I look out the window and see the rain. That point of focus might remind me that my body could use a glass of water. I drink a glass of water and a memory might pop up of my mother from childhood. That memory is projected from a chakra point and creates an emotional experience. Thoughts manifest into emotions that are either expressed or repressed. The directional momentum of those emotions determines what form is manifested or manipulated from the sound current created by either their release or capture.

We have been trained as a society to stifle our emotions. To fear anger and confrontation. To feel shame around crying and having tender moments. We have been taught that emotional pain is a weakness and should be hidden. That shoving your emotions down is a sign of strength. Have you ever wondered why shit might be hitting the fan in your life on repeat? Have you ever asked yourself how much more can you take? Have you ever thought that there might be more to life, but then second guess yourself and cave into outdated conditioned habits? Have you ever thought about why we have been conditioned in this way? What is the point of all of this?

We come to this planet as newborns crying and screaming to communicate, to have our needs met. Nature commanding nurture. Unbridled emotional expression is our first language as humans. The first sacred mantras that are chanted on repeat. The first songs of our people. Unapologetic poetry recited from a space of primal power. If this physical reality was created out of original sound, could it be that each soul that comes to the planet creates fresh and new realities from their original sound? So, what happened? Why have we been conditioned to silence our sound? Why have we been taught to turn our back on ourselves? Why is there a "medical diagnosis" for just about every form of emotional expression? Could it be to keep our power hidden from us? Could it be to prevent us from calling in the Golden Age?

A tremendous amount of power is generated from empowered emotional expression. The throat chakra and the sacral chakra are directly related to emotional expression, sound currents, creativity, purpose, and individuality. Both of these chakras are deeply connected. The throat chakra is located near the physical throat at the spine and the sacral chakra is located near the sex organs. If one is out of alignment or injured in any way it will greatly affect the other.

For centuries women have been tortured and killed for having the courage to release their sound and express their emotions. They have often been diagnosed with hysteria due to their emotional expressions. Throughout history, there have been a vast number of reasons why the hysteria diagnosis was given and hysterectomies were performed. One could have been that the dominating power generated by the empowered emotional expressions of Alpha Females taking accountability and remembering their mission was seen as a threat. These diagnoses and procedures took away a woman's primal power to be a portal to this planet and greatly affected their natural physical, emotional and hormonal experiences. It is possible that in many cases a hysterectomy procedure improves the quality of life. Yet I still can't help but wonder about the root of how they got to the hysterectomy in the first place.

In some cultures, female genital mutilation is still being performed to supposedly control a woman's sexual desires and make her more of a respectable woman. In some lineages, this barbaric procedure has been performed for centuries and is considered a normal tradition. According to these cultures, women that have not been altered by female genital mutilation are considered unsuitable for marriage, often seen as prostitutes, and cast out by their community.

If it interests you to get involved, I recommend researching organizations that are dedicated to stopping cultural violence such as female genital mutilation.

Women have been beaten down over time and manipulated into identifying with behaviors that are far from their potential. The power of accountability has been overshadowed by a false sense of duty to a role. In cultures all over the planet, if a woman obeys her husband she is called a good wife. If she stands her ground with her peers, she is called a bitch. That shit is so Piscean.

Men have not had it easy either. Male castration seems to date back to ancient times. There is a wild variety of reasons behind this barbaric ritual throughout its history. In some lineages, newborn babies had their testicles and penis removed. Keeping in mind the relationship between the genitals and the throat via the sacral and throat chakras, these procedures can drastically take the strength and power away from these humans. It can remove their source of creative force energy and alter their ability to use their body and sound current how they were intended to be used. The Roman Catholic Church is one of the more widely known participants that played a part in the castration of boys and young men for the sake of operas and oratorios. Women were banned from the Vatican, so they needed a specific sound frequency that apparently could only come from the Castrato for singing the "sacred" songs of the Catholic lineage.

To this day some men continue to be tortured for the sake of cultural norms or religious tradition. Men are physically and emotionally having their creative force power taken away from them at ages when they are too young to understand or speak up for themselves. Men are being brainwashed out of their loving and care-taking nature. These beautiful men on the planet are shoving down their emotions by the fistful to pass the test of being a "real man". My heart hurts for every little boy who played sweetly with baby dolls and was punished, who cried when he was in pain and got spanked for it, had a close and loving bond with another boy, and was labeled and called names. These boys have been continually conditioned out of organic expression.

If it interests you to get involved I recommend researching organizations that are dedicated to stopping religious abuse and violence.

Both men and women, masculine and feminine identifying and all other forms of identification, have potentially had their power, their creative force, their voice, and ability to communicate manipulated by an outside force. Why are arguably abusive traditions being passed down lineages without question in some cases? Why did we sign up to witness and go through this? Why did we choose this complex life? It's wild to consider that we did. Think about this though, when things are easy breezy and smooth sailing, we are less likely to dig deep and do the work. I believe that we signed up to face the effects of these atrocities because it is the contrast that creates the fuel in which we need to make huge changes and propel humanity and this planet into the Golden Age. We must do this step by step and support one another in the process.

We must find our voices. Healthy communication is one of the top points of focus for clients in many therapeutic practices. In my practices with my clients, it goes hand in hand with responsible emotional release work and deep accountability. People have forgotten their ability to communicate and express themselves because we have been manipulated out of our power for centuries. It is time to rise and use our sound to liberate ourselves and those whose voices are not being heard.

This highly orchestrated abuse that has occurred to both the masculine and the feminine has given way to so many organizations that promote a lack of accountability and irresponsible emotional expression and repression. Just take a quick look around. There is so much finger-pointing and judgment and blame going around. Waiting for someone else to do something about it and go first. We can do better than that. I can do better than that. I am doing better than that. By no stretch do I get it perfect. I have often created circumstances for myself to upgrade. One of the biggest muscles I have developed more recently is how to navigate people not liking me. Anyone who is in a space of leadership is going to have people really liking you, indifferent, and then just straight up loudly not into you. The Aquarian Age Leaders are coming to the table as highly sensitive and perceptive, which also means we are more vulnerable to psychic attacks. Strengthening your nervous system is highly recommended. Getting a dedicated daily alchemy practice is highly recommended. Responsible emotional release work is highly recommended. Accountability is highly recommended. Without these practices happening on the daily, leaders will get cut down to size and not fulfill their mission. I show up every single day to Kundalini Yoga, emotional release work, sound and movement therapies, mantra, and meditation. The time I spend on each might vary day to day, however, these practices are non-negotiable.

I am a living example of the power of this work, the power of my sound. I am here as a woman, a student, a teacher, a guide, a mother, and a full-on Alpha. I am dedicated to doing this deep work myself so I can pave the way for future generations to do the same. I am committed to walking the talk.

I would love to invite you right now to dig deep and feel into why you are here. Are you living up to your mission? Have you gotten beat down and now you believe the lies that take your power away? Did you let yourself get brainwashed and distracted from accountability? Have you bogged yourself down with backlogged emotions because you are scared to feel shit? These are the things we need to look at and get real with to even remotely have a chance to call in the Golden Age for our children and future generations. Are you willing to risk our children's future on this planet and beyond? Or are you ready to dig deep and show up?

This past year and a half I created the opportunity to transition my healing arts and Kundalini yoga practice to completely online and over the phone from home. During this time my baby girl witnessed my work. She witnessed mommy releasing her emotions through a variety of exorcises. She saw mommy actively taking accountability for her life every single day. She saw mommy helping other people who were ready to be brave and walk through the shadow. Mommy didn't go away to work any longer. Mommy was working at home together with her. Just like life happens with mommy at home together with her. She started to see mommy's work as an inclusive part of mommy's life with her. She started to see that mommy is very important to a lot of people. She then started to experience her remembering. In doing so, she is tapping into her importance and why she chose this life, her mission.

Then it happened.

"Mommy, I feel sad and scared. Can we do some of your work stuff together? I wanna punch the pillow and breathe and make noise."

I have been doing this work for a long time, both for myself and others. But it was that moment. The moment my courageous baby girl stepped into her power after witnessing mommy as an embodied guide. The moment I walked my baby girl through responsible emotional release and held my baby Alpha in my arms as she found her voice and trembled her nervous system into an upgrade. As she shed the caul of her outdated state of being, my baby girl harnessed her power and stepped onto her path supported and held by her mommy protector. That is the moment I witnessed a massive shift in my family lineage. That is the moment I truly became the teacher in the Golden Chain. Roughly two months after my teacher Guru Jagat made her way off the planet, I became the Alpha mommy teacher for my Alpha baby student.

The time is now to wake up. It is time to remember that we chose this life. That we chose choice. That we chose this mission to flex that choice. Now is the time to act. To release yourself from your emotional repression. To set yourself free and find your voice. To love your voice and find your power. To love your power and create a legacy. To create a legacy that has an impact on generations. To step onto the path to be a link in the Golden Chain of your lineage. Let us make our sacred sounds together right now, for ourselves and for those who no longer have a voice so that our future generations on this planet can be blissful.

Sources:

1. McVean, A. B. Sc. (2017, July 31). The history of hysteria. [Web page]. Retrieved from http://www.mcgill.ca/oss/article/history-quackery/history-hysteria

2. World Health Organization. (2020, February 3). "Female genital mutilation." Retrieved from http://www.who.int/news-room/fact-sheets/detail/female-genital-mutilation

3. Cheney, C.T. (2006). A brief history of castration. (2nd ed.)

ABOUT THE AUTHOR

BRANDY KNIGHT

Brandy Knight is the creatress of Inner Caulling LLC, her Life Coaching, Healing Arts and Kundalini Yoga practice. She is currently certified in modalities such as NLP, EFT, Law of Attraction, Hypnosis, Kundalini Yogic Science and Technologies and the list continues to grow. The driving force behind her practice is to guide others through responsible emotional release work and deep accountability so that they can step into their full power. Brandy strongly believes that we are here to propel and awaken our lineage while leaving a lasting high vibe impact with our legacy. When not tending to her practice, she is focused on setting the best embodied examples for her daughter. She cherishes being a mom above all else and relishes in the alchemy that this life experience has to offer.

innercaulling.com/
www.instagram.com/innercaulling/

7

CHANTEL PORTER

FROM THE ASHES OF THE PAST

Like a Phoenix, she rose from the ashes.

As a Self-Love and Rewilding coach, I work with women who want to heal their childhood and ancestral/generational trauma, shedding cultural conditioning, releasing their anger and coming home to themselves. I guide them to a place where they can see their innate worth and value, to a place of turning their pain into their power. We dig deep into the past and unearth what has been buried away for generations, setting not only her free but her ancestors as well. If you have never heard the term "Rewilding", think of it like returning a piece of land back to its natural state with all the animals that were there and the lushest beauty, but for women!

Generational trauma wasn't always the focus of my work, but as I healed my own trauma, I looked at all I had been through and overcame and I knew this would be my life's work. I released the shackles that had been placed on my lineage and set myself free. What really brought me here to this work though? The story that could show you that you're unbreakable, that nothing and nobody can ruin you unless you let them, that you are not the damsel in distress but the heroine of your own life. And, most of all, that you have everything you need inside of you to rise from the ashes of pain and darkness.

On March 11, 1989, the fire department arrived at our house to find a raging inferno in the basement, a fire started by children left unattended. Gary—the firefighter who saved me that day—shared with me his recollection of the events and I would like to share some of it with you.

"I remember we got the call, and when we arrived your mom was frantically yelling, "'The kids are downstairs", "The kids are downstairs." My partner Dale and I pulled off a hose line and headed for the back door to the basement, and we started crawling down the stairs. The smoke is really thick in basement fires and you can't see anything so it's all by feel. It was really hot too, so we didn't know if the stairs were burnt through or not. Luckily, the stairs were intact and we made it down, shooting water ahead of us. When we reached the floor, we started searching in a pattern from the wall that is a standard learned procedure while still spraying water at any flame visible in the smoke. I bumped into something and after feeling it, realized it was a couch so we felt our way around the couch and I was sweeping my arm back and forth and feeling on top of the couch. And then around it and in behind on the floor, I felt something. I took off my glove and felt it again, and it was a little arm—yours. I yelled at Dale, "I found one." We picked you up and then had to follow the hoseline back to find the stairs where we took you up and out and handed you over to some other firefighters and medics. By then, other firefighters had arrived and were fighting the fire. Because I knew where we had searched already, I went back downstairs and continued from the couch. I had no idea which child you were but I knew there was still one down there. I felt all around behind the couch again and then spread out further until I found a wall. As I felt down the wall, I found a doorway which turned out to be a bedroom. I started a right-hand search around the wall and found a bed but the mattress was pulled off of it. I felt all around it and then under it and found your brother. I doubled back with him and found the stairs and carried him up the stairs and outside where I ran with him towards an ambulance. That is when the Herald photographer took that picture you probably have seen since. I ripped off my air tank and mask and sat on the front lawn totally wiped, thinking, "Geez, I hope they are alive." The ambulances left with you and your brother in a hurry so I didn't know what your status was. The next shift, I got a hold of the medics who took you and asked how the two of you were. They said the little girl you brought out first got a lot of smoke and burns including her eyes; she is alive but they think she may be blind. My heart sank, then I asked how her brother was. They said, "Sorry Gary, he didn't make it". Wow, that really bummed all of the crew out, but especially Dale and I. So when I got that phone call from you, it was just super to know that you had come through and could see, and now that I saw the picture of you all grown up and pretty I think, OMG if I wouldn't have gone behind the couch until later in the search..."

The house fire was four weeks before my third birthday and eight weeks before my brother's fourth birthday, a life taken tragically and far too soon. Although I don't remember the fire or much of anything for some time after, what I do remember is my mother. A part of her died with my brother that day and it never returned. When I look at any pictures of her and I from after the fire, her lifeless and haunted eyes, her straight face, it almost smacks me in the face, even now. This is how I continued to experience her most of the time; this, or the anger that was almost always directed at me. I didn't understand it then, but the loss of my brother crippled her. It made parts of her close up completely and they became unavailable to me. The nurturing and reassurance I needed couldn't exist in the state she was in, especially when I was a daily reminder of the son she lost.

I can't remember what my mother was like before the fire but I know that her life had not been easy, she suffered great trauma and abuse before I was even born at the hands of her parents, relatives and others. The tragedy of the fire only added fuel to the raging fire of pain that burned inside her. Her pain would come out as rage, insults and abuse towards me. The abuse she suffered and her loss had mixed into the worst combination and she took much of it out on me and because of that her pain became my own as she tried desperately to get rid of it by throwing it at the closest person, me. But I believed if I tried harder she would love me, if I could do something right for once, maybe she would see me, instead of my brother, maybe she would light up when I entered the room instead of turn away.

As children who experience this type of trauma often do, I worked hard to please my mother, to be a good child, to not make her angry, to clean the way she wanted me to and to take care of my siblings without complaint. I wanted so desperately to take away her pain, but I was doing more as an eight-year-old than many adults are capable of doing. I began to assimilate myself with her in many ways in order to remain safe, but her anger, guilt and pain would prevent her from loving herself or me and grieving my brother.

When we merge with a parent because of trauma, we unconsciously share aspects of them, usually negative ones, from that parent's life experience. Then we repeat and relive certain aspects of their life in our own lives without understanding what is taking place. When I took on my mother's burden, I missed out on the experience of being given to, and that led to me having difficulty receiving from anyone, from relationships, from family, myself and from life itself. This created a pattern—a blueprint—for habitually feeling overwhelmed that I later passed on to my daughter.

And so, our tangled web of generational trauma and pain continued. The angry grandmother became the angry mother, who became the angry granddaughter. The dead son became the walking dead mother, who became the walking dead sister. I became the angry walking dead.

Generational trauma is the trauma that is passed down through generations of families. Because trauma affects genetic processes, anyone is susceptible to it. But specific populations are more susceptible due to their history of vulnerability in society, particularly those that endure repeated abuse, isolation, racism or poverty, or families that are impacted by tragedies, death, war, violence, rape, sexual assault, domestic abuse and hate crimes.

Generational trauma often shows up as hypervigilance, mistrust of others or the world, severe anxiety, depression, panic attacks, nightmares, insomnia, a sensitive fight, flight, freeze response, self-esteem and self-confidence issues. It may also manifest as a lowered immune system, health problems, and repeated patterns from family history. It will influence a person's beliefs about the world and themselves, their patterns, and behaviors. It will also have an impact on relationships, communication skills, decision making, jobs, personality, parenting and their overall view of the world around them.

It's often repeated on a seemingly never-ending loop that no one knows how to stop. It becomes an accepted part of a family's history due to being desensitized to the trauma, like an acceptance of fate; a family can become hopeless and feel powerless to stop it, and so it continues.

This is exactly what happened to my family. There was every form of abuse you could imagine. Alcohol and drug abuse, verbal, physical, and emotional abuse, as well as sexual abuse and rape. My mother moved out at a very young age and became a teen mom to my brother and I when she was fifteen and sixteen. We lived on welfare and my mother sold drugs to make extra money. She was involved with the Hell's Angels and spent much of her life running. She ran from her pain, her memories, her family, from the police and anyone else that challenged her to face her life.

As I grew up, I would boldly state, "I refuse to be like my mother; I will never do the things she did," and I believed this whole-heartedly. Many decisions I made when I was younger were strictly with that in mind, that I wouldn't end up like her. I didn't want to be a teen mom, so I waited to have sex. I finished highschool and went to college because she didn't. I barely drank and never did drugs. The thing about generational trauma though, you can have the best of intentions to be different from your family. But you cannot give to yourself or others what wasn't given to you unless you heal; otherwise the pattern only repeats. So, sure, on the surface it looked like I was doing all the right things to break the cycle, and to be honest, I did a lot of great things for myself, but trauma is a mofo, and let me tell you, I didn't really stand a chance against it all. The odds were *not* in my favor.

I didn't know how to receive or give love. I couldn't trust anyone and I thought I didn't matter in this world. I thought I wasn't capable of being like others, that the damage was too extensive, that I was too far gone to fix and so that would be my lot in life, to suffer and to be alone. I was carrying the trauma of generations of women before me, and I would go on to recreate much of it in my own life.

At the age of twenty-one, I lost a child tragically, like my mother had at 19. My entire world came crumbling down around me. I became a shell of a human and what anger was already present was only intensified. I lost all f*cks to be honest! I hated everyone around me who moved on and was happy, who didn't have to carry the pain I was in. I couldn't stand to be around anyone who was having children. I spiralled. I remember an aunt telling me in the hospital that I "was being punished for my mothers and my grandmother's sins." This only served to deepen my anger and pain. I was becoming my mother, and I was becoming my grandmother too.

I would go on to repeat many of the patterns and trauma that were passed down to me. A couple years after the death of my daughter, I became pregnant again but this time on purpose. Unbeknownst to me, it was just as my mother had after my brother's death. Insert generational trauma! The pain of losing my first-born daughter was so severe that all I could think of was having another baby. I didn't care what I had to do to get it. I could only see my own pain. This resulted in me accepting the unhealthy and abusive relationship with my daughter's father to get it, but something inside me was trying to come out. There was a voice inside that whispered to me that I needed to change, that I was meant for more, that I needed to protect my daughter. I didn't know it then, but I was hearing my soul calling to me, my inner knowing that was battling to crawl through the darkness I was in.

Unfortunately, it still wasn't enough yet. I was becoming a version of my mother that I swore I never would. My pain spilled out all over me and anyone who was close to me. I was a blazing wildfire on a wrecking path, incinerating everything I touched. I had hit my rock bottom and there was nowhere else to go. When my daughter was five, I finally realized that if I didn't do something about my life, I was going to end up harming my daughter in ways I swore I wouldn't, she would end up hating me as I had once hated my mother, and I would end up alone. There would be nobody who could change it; nobody could do it except me. It had to be me!

This realization burnt like the blazing fire that almost took my life. "If you can't handle the heat, get out of the kitchen" as the saying goes. Let me tell you, I became the heat but the heat that cooks your meal, not incinerates it! From that day forward, I radically changed my life, my daughter's life and the lives of many others around me because I decided to take responsibility for my life. I realized that nobody was coming to save me, nobody was coming to wave a magic wand that would make all my pain go away. I was the only one who could change my life, and that the control lay in my hands. To be honest that felt terrifying and empowering at the same time! I realized I didn't have to be a victim to my past, I was not the things that happened to me and they were not my fault but they were my responsibility to heal and release or it would all bleed onto my daughter. She didn't ask for this, she didn't deserve this!

I'm here to show you that you have a power inside of you to either start a wildfire or tame it. You have everything you need inside of you to heal anything that has happened to you. You do not have to be the victim, you can take your pain and turn it into your power, because nothing can ruin you unless you let it, NOTHING! I used to think I was a victim, that I was broken, never to be repaired. I believed my mother when she told me I was "a fuck up, just like my father". That was it, done, but I was wrong and so was she.

So, how do we heal generational trauma?

We have to talk about it openly and often. We need to shed our shame and guilt that has been placed on us by our society, churches, our families and the patriarchy. We need to find safe and inclusive spaces to learn about our past and our lineage. We need therapists and coaches who are educated on this topic to do this work with. We need to stop hiding from our friends, family, and our children what has happened, we need to stop sweeping things under the rug. We need to be open with the world so that others can see they're not alone. Because, when it cannot hide any longer, we can release the power it has over us and then we will rise.

We heal generational trauma by understanding what our ancestors went through and how the pain of neglect, death, trauma and so many other things impact us as humans. We get curious about our lineage and listen to their stories with compassion and acceptance. We release judgement and truly see them, reminding ourselves that had we lived a different life, had we lived their life and suffered as they had, we may have ended up in the same places, repeating the same patterns, causing the same pain. If we can put ourselves into another's shoes, as them, not as ourselves, then we can see and understand how people do what they do.

Having compassion and understanding for my mother and what happened in her life for her to say, do, act how she did is what helped heal me. It is what gave me an understanding of my own behaviors and showed me that it was not my pain to carry. It allowed me to see her as the wounded child she was that grew into the wounded woman, and it allowed me to cry for her. I still cry for her. I mourn the life she never had, the love she never got, and the relationship we never had. Most importantly, it allowed me to love her, fully and completely as she is, where she is, no matter what.

We can break free of the chains of our pasts, of society and all of its secrets and control. We can come together to give voice to our pains, to crack open the doors to our wounds and release what we have been carrying for generations that was never ours to begin with. We can rise together and generations will be healed, past present and future.

Like a Phoenix, she rose from the ashes.

Because not even fire can kill her!

ABOUT THE AUTHOR

CHANTEL PORTER

Chantel Porter is an Embodiment Coach and founder of the Wild Love Method. She feels a deep connection to the Earth, Moon and Womb. Chantel started Wild Woman Magick to guide women who struggle with cultural conditioning, generational, childhood and sexual trauma as she once did. Through Shamanic medicine, energy healing and positive psychology, she guides women back home to their bodies, their cycles and their wild nature. Chantel began this work after starting her own healing journey and realizing how little help there was for women in a way that wasn't dismissive, commercialized or a bandaid. She discovered how much power she had inside to heal herself and knew she had to share what she had learned with as many women as possible. She lives with her daughter, partner and their pets in British Columbia, Canada.

liinks.co/wildwomanmagick

8

HEATHER ROBINSON

THE MOUNTAIN

*R*eflecting on my journey and experiences, it can be frustrating for me that I didn't see things sooner or understand them earlier. It's somewhat disconcerting that this is where I'm at in my journey. I'm used to being vulnerable in many aspects, but it is uncomfortable to share this part of my world on these pages. Deep breath, and here we go.

I'm a single mom raising my son with the help of my parents in my childhood home. I had loads of trauma to heal postpartum. In my adult life I've healed much of my mother wound, and I moved through the remaining bits in my own journey to motherhood. Coming out of the deeply healing postpartum portal, I felt like I was close to the top of the mountain, moving beyond everything that had held me back. Then the fog cleared and, BAM, the father wound showed up and I realized there's still a huge climb left. One does not exist without the other, and they're both products of our lineage.

My son's father hates me and never wanted our child. He's expecting a child he actually desires before this book will be in your hands. I've repeated cycles and patterns to such an extent that my father thinks I ruined my life. He thinks I blame him for my failed relationships and that this is where I'm at in my life at age thirty-two.

It's hard to share all of that, because I guess somehow it means I failed. If your own father thinks so, it must be true right? Somehow being a single mom means I failed, I wasn't good enough, I wasn't desired. And then I watch my son at just twenty months old, confused why his cousin has a dad but he doesn't. It's hard because I know I'm not what some people think I am, and to me that means I've failed at being authentic.

I know these are all beliefs of others and not my own. They are the shadows of my experience trying to take hold. I gave these thoughts space to move through me, and then I remembered they're not mine. I'm not a failure in any capacity, no matter what anyone thinks, and I know and trust that my Dad spoke from a place of pain, he doesn't actually believe I'm a failure or ruined my life. Being a single mom and experiencing the things I'll share here in this chapter have absolutely changed my life for the better. They have transformed me and helped me grow and show up for myself and my son in a profoundly different way.

They've also helped me see and understand how I can choose what is true to me. I get to make choices, raise my son, and live in a way that is aligned with my values and authentic to my highest self. That's what the work I do is all about: feeling safe to be genuine and empowered to change the story.

My mission is to hold people as they heal deep wounds and empower them to choose a different path; to reprogram their default settings, heal their lineage, and live free from those bonds. This allows them to be free to be themselves, not what their stories tell them to be, and to feel safe in prioritizing themselves and their needs.

A while back, I found myself in the midst of a really high-energy moment with my son. Some would call it a breaking point. When parents are in these places emotionally or energetically, the fuse is almost non-existent. There is no patience, no more positive gentle parenting, no more chances. I hit my limit. In this experience, I witnessed myself. I was logically aware and conscious of how I was handling the situation, and I used my awareness and tools to talk myself down, adjust how I was moving through the experience, and resolve the conflict.

I was blindingly aware of the pattern of anger, frustration, and control. I was conscious of the shadows of my lineage's presence in that exchange.

I released it, took a deep breath, and went to calm my son down. Together, we co-regulated. I chatted with him while he breastfed. I lovingly explained what happened, apologized for getting upset, and set a boundary as his sniffles slowed.

I did it! I was breaking the pattern, healing my lineage, and choosing a different way. I was actively embodying what I teach and consciously evolving beyond some of the wounds my ancestors passed along.

Then, just as we were achieving a state of peace and calm together, the cycle came roaring back. My father walked up to me swiftly, and in his deep, serious, and controlling tone, finger pointed at me and all, he said, "I don't care what you've got going on, don't you *ever* take anything out on him ever again."

Astounded, I looked him straight in the eye and said, "Don't you ever tell me what to do with my child, *ever* again. And where the fuck do you think I got it from?"

As I held that mirror, repeating the cycle but attempting to break it all at once, I felt my blood boiling. I could logically see and witness, with pure consciousness and awareness, the pattern I had learned that I began to repeat with my child. I had caught myself and disrupted the pattern, and that I was reprogramming in my own system. I was proud of myself for doing that work and calming down quickly. I was proud of releasing my need to control my son to fit my story or needs in that moment. But to then witness the cycle desperately trying to survive, trying to control the situation, by controlling me, I was enraged. How dare my Dad tell me to not do exactly what he was doing in that exact moment! Was he blind? Did he not see? The cycle won when I reacted emotionally and I repeated it directly. Even though this time it was repeated as a mirror, that didn't make it any better. When I removed my son and I from the situation, my son was mortified. He perceived that his Papa was mad at him. My heart broke. I was so angry. I could see patterns and cycles of my lineage crystal clear, and I hated them.

I know no child will escape their upbringing unscathed. I know my son will have so much healing to do aside from anything I do. But I vowed, as a single mom, to make sure that I passed on as little as possible, because being unwanted by your father is a deep wound that I will hold him through as he grows. And to see how much work there was left to do on my side was incredibly defeating. It felt like I was looking up at a massive mountain that I thought I was close to the top of already.

Not having a father present in his life, I've done my best to be sure my son is surrounded by good men. My father, my brother, my neighbor, my friends. I want him to know divine masculine energy. But what happens when those men have their own issues, when the patterns and cycles are causing harm and creating wounds that will take lifetimes to heal?

I rolled up my sleeves, grabbed some tissues, and I got to work.

I began working with someone to guide me through deep inner child work as I moved through the custody journey with my son's father. I initially started because I wanted to be sure that there was nothing he could do or say in the process to get to me, and that I was completely healed from the experiences I had with him. No triggers. I also wanted to heal whatever caused me to attract toxic relationships to begin with, and at the very least, heal my side of things that I'll be passing on to lessen the load on my son, making his mountain of healing smaller. That's the goal as parents, right? To make the next generation better, more whole, happy, and healthy?

I began to see that the issue wasn't what I thought it was. It wasn't a toxic ex. It wasn't a streak of bad luck. It wasn't a fluke of falling pregnant with a manipulative narcissist. It was a cycle. It was a pattern. It was my lineage I was living out. This healing work began to show me that my relationship with my son's father was a direct reflection of my relationship with my own father, as were many other previous relationships. What I left when I packed up my life and moved across the country seven months pregnant was also waiting for me at home. To be clear, they aren't alike at all as individuals, but the aspects of the relationships I have with them are very similar: control, manipulation, shame, conflict. There is no escaping your shadows. There is no escaping your lineage. There is only consciously evolving beyond them, and you'll continue to repeat the patterns until you do.

So, I had a really deep, emotional exchange with my father to let him know how I felt. I shared with him my new understanding of things, what I felt the issue was between us, and the aspects of how we interact that don't work and don't feel good for either of us. I asked him to help me heal the relationship so I could teach my son what it's supposed to look like. I want to teach him what resolution looks like, that conflict isn't something you ignore, avoid, or run away from, and that big emotions aren't scary. I want to show him that people can unknowingly hurt you and you can meet them with compassion. I don't want my son to see a strained relationship between his Mama and Papa, or even his Mama and Father.

In my work guiding mother wound healing, I've learned that wounds, especially mother wounds, often form when we perceive as a tiny human that we aren't loved unconditionally. But this is our birthright and innately expected from our mothers. This then translates to feelings and beliefs of being unworthy, undeserving, and in some way wrong, bad, or broken. These programs and stories follow us throughout our lives and can manifest in many different ways. The cure is to stop seeking unconditional love outside of self, as we expected it to initially come from our mothers, and begin to mother ourselves by loving ourselves unconditionally. This includes prioritizing Self in a drastically different way.

The patterns that repeated with my failed relationships are rooted in my experiences and learnings from my lineage. Mother wounds, father wounds, ancestral wounds, patterns, cycles, traumas, shadows, and programming—they're all incredibly powerful in the foundations of our growth and being human. Everyone may become conscious of these things at different points, and motherhood was that turning point in my own journey. Parenthood brings up an awareness of our childhood that provides fertile ground for healing and growth of one's inner child and lineage. Some of those patterns in my lineage that end with me are control, manipulation, anger, avoidance of conflict and resolution, and a lack of emotional intelligence and presence.

I didn't have much control over my life or experiences as a child, and it's vital for a tiny human's development and autonomy to trust them and give them some control of their world. It has translated for me as an adult into a lack of trust in myself, and a strong resistance to any outside control. In relationships, that looks like stubbornness, rigidity, and a lack of compromise. My son's father used manipulation in an attempt to control my life and decisions to suit his desires, and this triggered me deeply. My own parents, and the majority of their generation, unknowingly attempt to control behavior by saying, "Don't do that," "Stop crying," or, "You're fine." They instill a lack of trust by saying, "Be careful," "You're going to get hurt," or flat-out dismissing feelings.

It's really easy when children don't do as you wish to try to shame, guilt, or manipulate them, and then get angry when none of it works. The cycle of anger I've witnessed throughout my family, in multiple generations, was not something I thought I carried. But becoming a mother showed me that it just takes the right circumstance and trigger, and I recognized the patterns of my lineage at the root of it all. When space wasn't held for my big emotions as a child, when I wasn't validated for being upset when I had no control in something, I grew up with a lack of emotional intelligence to hold space for my son's big emotions.

I quickly became conscious of this short fuse and its root and began working to expand my capacity. This requires a lot of self-love, self-care, and prioritizing myself and the things that fill me up and bring me joy. Prioritizing not only my needs but also my desires is a key component of this work. Caring for myself first and mothering my inner child has transformed my ability to take care of others. In giving myself unconditional love, I can pass it along to my son.

I am very adamant about healing these shadow aspects as I raise my son and have been teaching my own parents these things as well. I don't want anybody to control, manipulate, or shame him. I also don't want his feelings invalidated or brushed aside like they don't matter. I definitely don't ever want him to perceive that he isn't loved unconditionally. When the expectation is set that he's his own human with his own desires, preferences, and ideas of things, I can approach him as a person and surrender my own desires to validate him and compromise, within bounds, and we can both move forward happily.

This is a form of conflict resolution I taught myself. As a child, I never really witnessed resolution, and then I was confused when I attracted relationships that lacked it as well. As a result, I've always pushed people beyond their capacity, not honoring their need to take space to cool off or trusting they'd come back to resolve it, and I'd further escalate the conflict seeking resolution from someone desperately trying to escape it all.

I am consciously breaking this pattern in the moments of tension with my son, and now my father as well. It's not always feasible to walk away and cool off with a toddler, but a quick deep breath, a release, and a switch in tone usually does wonders to move forward to resolution. I'm proud to be the one to break this cycle.

My son will have so much healing to do because his soul knows his father wanted an abortion. I do believe my son chose this life and his parents though. He chose his lineage, his father wound, the relationship he will have with his father, and that mountain of healing he will climb. He also chose me to hold him through it, because I'm paving the way for him. He chose me because I'm conscious of it all and doing my part, both in my own lineage and for others.

The work I do and the healing I hold people through is profound. On a small scale it can seem really simple—to prioritize yourself and reparent yourself by giving yourself unconditional love, finding joy and pleasure in life, and playing and having fun. But the larger picture is healing lineages by consciously evolving beyond the programming. If we're aware of the cycles and patterns playing out, and the wounds that are controlling how we move through life, we can then choose differently and take our power back.

It's not an easy process, and it's not a quick one, but it is incredibly transformative. Reprogramming our defaults bit by bit, by simply choosing to love ourselves first is so simple, yet so fundamental. My work helps people whose programming, beliefs, and stories are holding them back in their lives. These cycles and patterns prevent them from achieving their desires and living their dreams, and so we work to remove the blocks, bring awareness to the wounds, and integrate the shadows. Utilizing the mother archetype, I bring in the elements of unconditional love, joy, pleasure, and play as they heal, re-parent themselves, and learn to care for themselves in a radically different way.

In this process they heal, break cycles, and access unconditional love for themselves and others. Their default settings shift, and they no longer find themselves repeating the same stories. They often find their relationships grow, experiences become more fulfilling, and the way they walk through life becomes more confident and empowered.

As we all move through our lives and navigate the baggage that we didn't know we had and begin to see the world and our experience in it more clearly, we each have a choice to do something about it and change the course of our lineages. All it takes is conscious evolution, to stay aware, consistently make a different choice, and evolve beyond the negative cycles of our ancestries. We can honor and celebrate the wisdom and teachings that still serve us and also free ourselves from the bonds of the past and make our own mark in the lineage. We are free to be ourselves, make our own choices, and live a life we desire.

So, I invite you today, to first take stock of your life and how you move through it. Bring your consciousness to how you feel, and just notice. Then, tap into joy, play, fun, pleasure, bliss, and most importantly, unconditional love. How would you, and your inner child, feel to receive these things right now?

ABOUT THE AUTHOR

HEATHER ROBINSON

Heather Robinson is a guide for mother wound healing and conscious evolution. She is a mentor for women and mothers to expand in all aspects of life by teaching them how to integrate the spirit and unconditional love of the mother archetype. By prioritizing sacred self-care, embodiment, and conscious awareness, Heather empowers women with the tools they need to consistently show up for themselves. The embodiment of the mother allows her to show up for herself, her son, as well as her clients in a deeply nourishing way. Her mission is to help others heal their ancestral wounds, break the harmful patterns and cycles of their lineage, and access freedom by consciously choosing a different way every day.

www.iamhro.com
www.instagram.com/iam_hro/

9

LINDSAY RAE D'OTTAVIO

BREAKING GENERATIONAL GUILT

I am a Jewish woman. I was raised in a very reformed household in a religious sense, but culturally, being Jewish was a massive part of my identity growing up. It is still something I am proud of—despite the fact I could never complain when I was younger because my mother would remind me her father fought in WWII to free our people, who suffered more unimaginably than I could ever fathom! Don't even get me started on the guilt of Egypt!

"Jewish Guilt" is real, and this layer of shame would go on to lay on top of every aspect of my youth until my mid-thirties. The shame was like a slimy film that never felt like it belonged to me. I was thirty-two when I got my first tattoo, despite begging for one since I was eighteen because my mother would say things like, "Do whatever you want but you cannot be buried with our family." In our family, the guilt continued even past death.

The Holocaust was only one way my mother would use guilt to manipulate me. This generational curse would find its way into all aspects of how she parented me. She would shame me for everything, from asking for lunch money to the way it made her feel that I didn't care about myself (or her) when I refused to wear makeup.

My father on the other hand went through a midlife crisis around forty years old. I was thirteen at the time. He chose to abandon his family, convert from Judaism to a Messianic born-again Christian and marry a recovering alcoholic woman with six kids. The life they modeled and the words they preached were completely incongruent. From him I'd receive guilt from things like my mom asking for child support, my weight and not going to Church. Shame became his way of exerting control over me. Guilt, shame and physical intimidation were so normal growing up that when I would go to my friend's homes, I expected screaming, flying objects and slamming doors...only to find that was most certainly not normal.

It was not until I was in my twenties that my mother finally let me in on some of my dad's secrets. They revealed childhood sexual abuse, violence and addiction from his family of origin. I was finally able to understand that the way my father copes was the way his father coped, and the way my brother, sister and I cope with trauma.

We were essentially raised to believe that the only way to make someone do what you want is to shame them into feeling terrible about themselves.

This is a form of Generational Violence. A lifetime of guilt paired with physical and emotional intimidation and violence. My first suicide attempt was at sixteen years old. At this point, my mom kicked me out of her home for talking to my father who had left us homeless to be with his new wife. This is the trauma that is passed down from father to son to daughter. This is the generational curse that stops with me.

When my daughter was born, I made a vow to be an opposite parent than how my parents treated me. I vowed to never yell, to teach her about choices along with the consequences and rewards of her choices. I raise her that the best way to make mommy proud is to "Be the best *you* you can be."

I had an opportunity to see the fruits of my inner work recently with my eight-year-old daughter. She had trashed her room. I mean literally piles of toys and books and clothes all over her floor, her drawers open with clothes spilling over the edge—and don't even get me started with the gross food plates she would hide behind other messes. For the first time in eight years of being a mom I felt actual anger towards my child. I was so mad at her disrespect of her things that I cried, because I refused to yell and the emotions were so intense. She, for the first time ever, came on her own, wrapped her arms around me and said, "Mama, I am so sorry," and then began to clean her room.

At first, I was so proud I didn't yell. Then I realized that guilting my child with tears may not have been my father's tactics, but they were certainly my mother's. I took five minutes to practice my 4-7-8 breathing (video to this linked in my QR code at the end of my chapter for your own self practice) to bring my heart rate down and went back upstairs to apologize to her. I said to her "Mommy should not have cried and made you feel guilty and I am sorry. Mommy has not been setting the best example for how to keep our things clean so I am going to go clean right now too. If you complete your cleaning, you can still have your playdate and if you don't, you will be choosing no technology for three days. It will be your choice because you have two options, which means if you choose not to clean mommy will enforce the no technology consequence...what choice do you want to make, Gaia?" Her response? "I choose to clean."

In one single instance of parenting, I was able to re-parent my own inner child. I set a new path forward for my bloodline. One that shows how to communicate, how to take ownership when you are wrong and how to follow through. She was able to weigh her options and make a decision for herself without guilt, shame or intimidation.

This is what *we* get to do differently as parents. This is why I am a full believer that the generation of children that we are raising are going to be the ones that will save the world. We are coming from such a different place in raising these children who are trauma-informed and kinder. Most importantly, as my generation becomes parents ourselves, we are not being jerks to our kids, because we know how it feels and we've made the choice to change the pattern.

I have a video of my daughter, from my thirtieth birthday at the hotel we were staying in. She was three years old at the time. The video shows her looking in a gigantic mirror and repeating, "I am beautiful.. I am empathetic. I am smart. And I am kind." I watched myself on the screen ask her what empathetic means? She plainly says, "Empathetic is when you can feel how other people feel." It is such a simple concept that a three-year-old can understand it, yet so many adults struggle with it because it was never taught.

We as a society have failed to teach empathy. We assume that you are supposed to be born with it. However as I broke my own generational curses, I have come to believe that empathy is taught and then intrinsically grows within you.

We exist in a constant state of worrying about what other people think about us. Years and years of breaking down modesty practices have caused shame to become a normal feeling within ourselves. But shame and guilt breed anger. We project our emotions onto others rather than reading their emotions for what they are. We assume what other people feel and what other people think based on our own pasts rather than taking the time to empathize.

As I have gotten older, I have gotten better about being able to say things to advocate for my emotional needs. Example, I will say to my partner, "I am having a really insecure day. I do not feel good about myself today. Can you love me a little louder?"

A tool we use to ask for empathy in our home is the phrase, "Can you love me louder?" It does not mean tell me you love me a million times. For me, loving me louder means you see me and acknowledge where I am emotionally and offer words of kindness and affirmation.

Knowing where you stand in your own personal emotions is the only way that you can advocate for yourself and ask for what you need. For years, I would take someone else's bad day, internalize it and selfishly project it back on the other person as if they had an issue with me. If we do not advocate for our own needs, we will fall back on our genetic instinct of reacting how we watched our elders react when we were being raised. It is highly unfair to expect our partners, staff, colleagues or family to magically know what we need; no human can actually read minds.

The best example of when I learned to self-advocate was when I would be having an insecure day and needing attention, but was not asking for it. I was just expecting it and then getting mad at my partner when it was not delivered exactly to my expectations, despite the fact I had never taken the courtesy to even let him know what that expectation was. Sounds an awful lot like someone else I described earlier in this chapter, huh?

I was not getting what I wanted because I never asked for it. It is the spiral, which happens in not just romantic relationships, but interpersonal relationships, business relationships, even familial relations.

Generational curses are not broken overnight. Genetic instinct is ingrained in each of us and reprogramming our brains to ignore instinct is a daily practice. It is difficult to put your ego to the side, to accept that you may need help. When you do and you are able to find the right people to help you, you are actually giving yourself more power. In the past I didn't want to learn or evolve because I felt like I was behaving the same way everybody else around me was behaving and how my elders had behaved before me. This made me inauthentic, and drove home the shame I was raised with and the feelings of never being good enough. I have learned as an adult that different people excel in different areas. To have a well-rounded personal and professional life, you need people who are experts in their area to feed you knowledge and to teach you and to help you learn. Choosing to do the work of learning how to respond instead of react has been the catalyst for my growth.

Learning to sit with my thoughts and face them without fear has been one of the greatest challenges of my existence. I have put in the practice of reprogramming my brain to ask myself important questions like, "Why are you feeling this?" and "What do you want from this?"

Nobody asked me why I got divorced when I first announced I was leaving my husband and moving into my photography studio. But I believe that it is a really important question to ask a person. Choosing that full commitment to myself was one of the most difficult things I have ever done. I had stayed in the wrong relationship for ten years. Luckily, I left earlier than my parents split following twenty-seven without love.

Unlike my dad, my ex-husband is a great guy and an incredible father. But he was the wrong partner for me. He is a person who did not support my growth, who did not see big picture ideas, and fueled my self-doubt on my ability to be a business owner. Being married to my ex was like being married to a computer system. That is who he is, the coder, the computer guy. While I would be having big dreams and lofty ideas of things that I wanted to accomplish and who I wanted to be, he'd have me constantly questioning my reality; for him, if it was not coded on the computer, it wasn't a human possibility. He left me emotionally empty and put up walls that stretched from heaven to hell that I could never break through. I was more alone while partnered for ten years than single, despite rarely being physically alone.

The struggle was real for me to quiet my own inner voices and quiet the actual voices of people who say that you were supposed to stay together for your children and, "Do it for the kids."

I finally realized I can respect my ex-husband, I can respect my child, and I can respect myself while still leaving, and simultaneously have a positive co-parenting relationship and thriving business that helps women find confidence. I think one of the things that draws my clients to me is the fact that I'm very vulnerable about my own journey, and my own challenges with self-love, my own struggles with confidence, and my own mission to change my future from the path of my past. Through this vulnerability and openness, I have connected to incredible women in my work that catapult my own evolution. I am now able to look at someone and find something beautiful in anybody. I wanted to prove that every woman can be beautiful, no matter who she is, how old she is, what her skin color or ethnicity is, that she has beauty in her. This is something my parents simply could not do.

My parents' divorce was emotionally, spiritually and physically violent and lasted for ten years before being finalized. I would be brought to different lawyers, handed from parent to parent and used like a pawn on a chessboard for my mother and father to attempt to hurt each other.

When it came time to finally self-advocate for my own peace and move out of my beautiful home, I weighed my choices and took the leap of believing in myself enough to know that I could start from nothing. I was not forced to be with a man for twenty-seven years like my mother did.

I did the internal work to believe in my personal power again and build myself back up. When I actually got legally divorced I called my ex-husband and I said, "I have gotten so much healthier. I'm sorry that you had the sickest version of me, the person who could not respond through any other lens but trauma." Something, again, my parents simply could not do.

I now consistently and religiously take stock of the people in my life. This doesn't mean I don't value you or think you're an incredibly beautiful, wonderful soul. What it means is that the energy that I'm receiving needs to be tailored to my emotional needs and what I am trying to do as a woman, as a mother, as a girlfriend. If something someone says or does doesn't fit into my mission, then there is room on the outside layers of my energy, like the rings of Saturn. I, however, choose to curate who is closest to me and my source of energy. The humans in my life now are striving to make their own successful businesses, are supporting each other, are trauma informed and will speak your name in a room full of opportunity.

Another curse-breaking tool I use is to pause before I respond to someone rather than allowing my genetic instinct to lead my current life. When you pause before you respond, you're actually responding to someone's intention versus reacting through the lens of your own past experiences. The pause allows you to gather composure. During the pause time, my heart rate slows and I'm able to gain perspective on my nervous system and my generational instincts to be able to make a decision instead of a reaction.

I love that the words "trauma-informed" are becoming widespread and popular. Being trauma-informed, does not mean that you have gone through trauma; it means that you understand that people have gone through things, and they might be replying to you out of their past experiences rather than out of the present moment. Being able to have a trauma-informed perspective, not just for yourself but for others, will completely change the way that your relationships function.

I was crying to my boyfriend one day about my mom not answering her phone for over a month. She didn't want to talk to me because I asked her to refrain from sharing information about my life with my estranged father. He reminded me that my mother suffered the same trauma I did and then some. I can clearly hear his Long Island accent as he said to me, "Lindsay, look at all the trauma you went through and you were only with your dad until you were nineteen. Your mom was with him for twenty-seven years. That is eight more years of trauma that she went through with the same man, and yet you expect her to reply to you without that perspective. You want me to give you grace when you forget to pause and react instead of respond, but you are not giving her the same grace." It all shifted for me with that single statement.

This is the work of breaking generational trauma. Small consistent choices on how *you* respond to the world around you. Having a trauma-informed approach to life won't only change

how you deal with yourself, but it will completely transform your relationships with every other person in your life.

Will you react the same way your parents and their parents before them did or will you take active steps to break the cycle and learn to respond to the present?

While still honoring my boundaries and growth I am able to finally forgive my mother. I am able to finally say the words, "I do not blame you anymore, you were a victim too. The things that you would say and do to me were because you were afraid too."

ABOUT THE AUTHOR

LINDSAY RAE D'OTTAVIO

Lindsay is an internationally published multi-award-winning photographer and Inspirational Speaker. She earned first place at RangeFinders Celebrate the Body and first place at one of the world's largest speaking competitions, the 2021 Speaker Slam on Self-Acceptance. Lindsay owns and operates Self Love Experience out of Troy, New York. She is an active contributor to Women's Business Daily and Co-Author of the Amazon International Best-Seller Success Codes: The Secrets to Success You Weren't Taught In High School which won a 2021 International Impact Award. From a difficult upbringing with a family on welfare to building a multiple six figure business. Lindsay's focus is on self-love, self-confrontation, overcoming body insecurity and seeing yourself as more than scars of your past.

Lindsay believes confidence in the skin you are in trickles into every aspect in your life and gives women permission to feel beautiful exactly as they are.

www.flowcode.com/page/thebodyimageactivist
www.instagram.com/thebodyimageactivist/

LYNDSEY HARPER

THE BIRTH OF AWAKENED SOULS

I never thought I wanted to have kids. As a young adult, I
didn't babysit and I was never really around young kids
or babies. When I was around babies, I would almost feel disgusted
like I had a strong aversion to them. As I got older and discussed
future plans and desires with my partners, I never painted a picture
that I wanted kids. I always figured it was because my parents were
divorced and I had my own baggage around marriage and family.
Looking back now, I can see how most of my life I was operating
from a "not-self" space. I was living in the low vibration or
expression of myself. I wasn't acting authentically, instead trying to
do things I thought I "should" do or be someone I thought others
wanted me to be. I honestly didn't think there was any other way to
operate, and was totally unaware of any tools out there that could
help me. It wasn't until I met my now-husband and had our first
child that I felt something was seriously wrong with me. It was more
than postpartum depression; it felt like a spiritual awakening and

identity crisis all in one. I needed answers, I needed information, and I needed more out of life, so I started searching.

Once I found Human Design, I finally had a system and language that could explain why I felt how I felt and gave me a roadmap for healing. I could see that I had this potential fear of having dependents activated in me, consciously and subconsciously. It was right there in my chart! I felt validated and felt like I finally understood who I was.

Knowing what I know now, especially from the Human Design System, I can see very clearly where much of my childhood pain and baggage came from. I can see how I operated for so much of my life in this "not-self" space. I was out of alignment, and inauthentic. Moving through life in this way seemed to point me in the wrong direction, my trajectory was slightly skewed; my timing felt off and everything felt so hard. I was constantly asking myself and others what I "should" do. That word "should" often brings a person up in the mental space, listing out reasons to go left or right; struggling to feel secure in the correct decision. Ever since I was in school, I can remember parents and teachers telling me to think through it, use my brain, think with my head. But the majority of us aren't designed to make decisions mentally; most of us are meant to use our bodies.

There are many sayings that sound something like: "The universe always tries to knock you back into alignment with your highest self." While this rings true, we can't escape the mechanics of our energy. The specific geometry of our cells and the innate wisdom we hold within our core. I felt this most with the birth stories of both my children, which spanned from an unconscious conception perspective with my first that awakened my inner power to an expansive and conscious experience with my second.

When I became pregnant with my first child, I was completely changed forever. Something deep inside of me awakened. It was like I had never truly known myself or my body before that. I intuitively gravitated towards learning about the natural birth process, but was scared shitless of actually giving birth. With my lifestyle at the time, you would have thought I'd say "Give me all the drugs!!" But there was a calling from deep inside to know more, ask more questions, and attempt this natural experience. And through the heartburn, muscle aches and pain, I discovered a newfound love of my body and all that it could do. For the first time that I could remember, I started listening to my body. I felt powerful, capable and divine.

When the contractions started to intensify and it was time to go to the hospital, I went completely inward. Was that good or bad? I still don't really know and I'm not sure if that's even a valid question. I internalized all the shock, fear, excitement and pain. It became an out-of-body experience that was both the most traumatic and beautiful event I have ever gone through.

I had put so much preparation into the labor and delivery. Birthing techniques like hypnobirthing, using ice, different breathing exercises and basic prenatal yoga, all came to me through lots of reading! I felt like I had as much of a handle on it as I could. Luckily I was able to have a smooth birth, no drugs, and delivered my daughter after about five hours at the hospital. The pushing was by far the hardest, but what I wasn't prepared for was the after.

My beautiful baby was on my chest and I was in excruciating pain. I could feel the burning, stinging, slicing sensation of the stitching from where I tore. The doctor took forever to stitch me up and the pain was so intense, I was barely aware that I was holding my baby let alone trying to establish our bond. My expectation of that moment was what I gathered from movies and not real life: a mother tired but filled with tears of joy and bliss. I was tired, and I was happy my baby was there, but the emotions weren't there yet. I was in too much pain and shock. I felt like I had been hit by a Mack truck. My eyes were swollen shut because I had pushed so hard I popped the blood vessels in both eyes. I had the nurses and OB-GYN poking and prodding me so much I couldn't be *present* in the moment with my daughter.

I had the natural childbirth I wanted, yet I felt disconnected from it. I had prepared and worked so hard to accomplish this smooth beautiful birth, so why did I feel so apart from it? It's true that nothing ever really goes according to plan –and there are so many aspects of this process that a birthing class doesn't cover!

Little did I know about the afterbirth, which honestly was the most traumatic part of the entire pregnancy and birthing experience. But it also played a major role for me to go deeper into the studies of natural childbirth and detoxing from medication. I learned about the techniques my doula used to cope with the pain, and she held me in support during the entire delivery. It was amazing to have that type of guidance during the birth of my daughter, and I wish all women had it. But what I really wish I had was support after the birth. Because there are some things I had to learn the hard way.

Did you know most hospitals have a best practice to administer Pitocin after the baby is born, in order to prevent blood hemorrhage and aid in the delivery of the placenta? I had no idea; I thought I had given the directive of no drugs. But I was administered Pitocin without my knowledge and without consent, to only later find out through my medical records. So, why does this matter?

Pitocin is often given to induce labor or increase the contractions. It's a synthetic hormone that also affects the oxytocin hormone production. That's our feel-good, natural morphine, cuddly, loving hormone that promotes the bonding with baby and strengthens the breastfeeding journey. If this drug is used as a best practice in almost all hospital births, and the rates of postpartum anxiety and depression and the struggles with breastfeeding are increasing, could there be a correlation here? It was at this point my internal radar was going off inside me. My investigator/martyr archetypes needed more information, more research, and to try things for myself to find out what does and doesn't work.

From there I discovered homeopathy and started studying detoxes. After feeling a great depression within my being and having serious bouts of inflammation and body rashes, I discovered this could be due to the Pitocin. So I did a homeopathic detox. The remedy was created from the drug Pitocin itself. The energetic frequency medicine worked like a magnet, drawing the remainder of what existed in my system on a deep cellular level.

There was so much that felt unnatural during my first childbirth experience, even though I had prepared and tried to gain as much education as possible about natural childbirth. It was shortly after my daughter's birth that I started to identify as a sacral being. I came to understand that I was designed to use my sacral energy center to be my decision-making guide. I started to feel an expansion near my gut when something was a "yes" for me and felt a clenched retraction when something was a "no". I could actually feel my own consistent energy and where it wanted me to go.

As I dove deeper into studying Human Design, I started 'living my own experiment', as the HD community calls it. I followed my internal sacral response and let this feeling of expansion in my gut lead me on a path that helped me discover more about childbirth and parenting. It also led me on a journey of Kundalini yoga conscious conception, pregnancy, childbirth and postpartum, as well as homeopathy school. It was fascinating to learn how these systems and technologies worked harmoniously together. Weaving Human Design, with Kundalini yoga and homeopathy was proving to be very powerful.

Homeopathy immediately resonated for me, in its common sense. I loved the concept of the "like cures like" philosophy. I could look at a Human Design chart to see how the mechanics of the energy works, where there could be imbalances or blocks, then use the Kundalini yoga and homeopathy to restore balance and remind the body how to heal. This knowledge opened up a whole new level of natural childbirth.

I had access to remedies that immediately helped with the heartburn, instead of a daily pill which increases risk for certain cancers and decreases bone density. There were remedies to help with breech baby position, ease contraction pains, strengthen contractions, help with blood loss, and so many other issues that arise when pregnant and in labor. I felt much more prepared for all aspects of my next labor and delivery. I also trusted my sacral response to guide me.

My second pregnancy was much harder on me emotionally and physically. I was chasing after a two-and-a-half-year-old toddler at the height of a worldwide pandemic. The amount of tense, fear-driven energy surrounding me on a daily basis was a lot to handle. I remember using the remedy aconite a lot to just deal with the shock of everything happening in the world, and I created a flower remedy called "the weight of the world" which helped my emotions greatly. The Kundalini yogic teachings for pregnancy were life-changing and supportive for each trimester. Just doing five to eleven minutes a day of the *Adi Shakti* meditation was grounding and powerful.

I'll impart a couple teachings that I found to be so sacred and beautiful, as every woman should have access to this knowledge if it calls to them...

Have a 120-day celebration. This is when the soul enters the body. Make it a priority to have a very beautiful, blessed and sacred day. Surround yourself with good company, food and meditate. It's a day to focus on raising your vibration to call in the most aligned and high soul. I celebrated this day with a small group of friends. We did yoga, some meditation and shared poems, songs and sweet blessings. I felt so honored and held by my sisters on that day. I felt a very strong soul come in and the main phase that came to me over and over that day was "agent of change".

Chanting mantras like "Adi Shakti" helps increase emotional intelligence for the males, brings forth more creative, less self-centered, and more intuitive traits in many aspects of life. The "Pootaa Maataa Kee Asees" is a mantra you can play during pregnancy and throughout childhood to invoke protection around the child. The mantra "Akal" helps the soul adjust and is important to play in the background after birth to ease the transition.

So, on Easter Sunday, our son was born. He was actually a couple of days late, and I was eager to meet him. But when it was finally showtime, he didn't waste any time. I started contractions while taking a bath with my daughter around 7pm that evening. I figured we would probably go to the hospital in the morning, but I listened to my body and knew things were moving fast. I remember thinking on the way to the hospital, "If we get to the hospital and they say I'm only 6cm dilated, there's no way I can do this without drugs!!"

When we got to the hospital, it was 12:40am and I could barely walk; they rushed me up to labor and delivery, and got me on a gurney to check me out. The nurse yelled out, "She's totally complete! Get her to a room!" From there they told me to start pushing on the gurney, and in a few pushes he was out. I did it—without drugs! I was relieved and shocked at how fast everything was going. And where was my baby?? They said he was having trouble breathing with lots of fluid from the speedy delivery. I was so scared! I needed to see him, I needed to be with him, I needed to play "Akal". Once he was in my arms and okay, I finally got my moment and it was wonderful.

This "agent of change" graced us quickly with his shocking and provoking energy.

This time around, the midwife honored my request and allowed me to deliver the placenta naturally with no Pitocin. She coached me through some simple breathwork and relaxation techniques that made the delivery of the placenta quick and painless. For some reason, my body was shaking out of control, as if anticipating the pain I was about to endure from the stitching. This time the midwife assured me that what I had experienced before was not normal and she wouldn't have me go through that again. She was right. She did such a great job, administered the right local anesthetic and was gentle and quick. It was a totally different experience.

Neither birth went exactly as planned. Each had its own surprises, challenges and fears. And each served a pivotal role in my awakening and expansion. To have a conscious and present second pregnancy and birth was such a gift. I learned through trial and error from my first pregnancy, while letting my body command my decisions to lead me to a more aligned experience with my second pregnancy. I had to see to believe and experience what didn't work and what worked for me in order to share this.

As I dive deeper into the sphere of parenting, I have to admit the same rules apply. I listen to my sacral response. I let it guide me in terms of what I need and what my children need. It never leads me astray. And when I get overwhelmed, allow myself to get wrapped up in the mental space, or try to force myself to follow a feeding or sleeping schedule because I think certain rules "should" work for me and my family, somehow it often leads to frustration. And when that frustration hits, I tell myself to go back to the basics. Get back to my sacral, use the yoga and a remedy to help me get rid of a block or move through emotions with more grace. I ultimately keep teaching myself how to communicate with my own soul, and nothing feels more powerful than that.

I had to give birth to my children in order to rebirth myself, understand myself and trust myself. That took over thirty years of many trials and errors while living out of alignment from my authentic self. But what if our children grew up encouraged to deeply understand and listen to themselves? Would they endure less pain through early adulthood? Could they be more "successful"? Would there be a higher level of potential they could achieve?

I believe the world would have less angry, bitter, disappointed and frustrated people if we understood ourselves earlier and lived with less resistance. If I can learn to live out my design and teach my children to do the same, then I'm hopeful a lineage of radical self-acceptance can be passed onto future generations.

ABOUT THE AUTHOR

LYNDSEY HARPER

Lyndsey Harper founded her human design and Homeopathic counseling practice in 2018. She works with women who want to step into their true matriarchal roles. She teaches mothers and soon-to-be mothers to use human design and homeopathy to deeply understand themselves and heal their physical, mental and emotional bodies. Lyndsey's programs are designed to give women the knowledge and tools to have the conscious experience they desire from pregnancy to parenthood. These women emerge as leaders, equipped to help the entire family unit resolve chronic patterns and deeply connect to one another. After the birth of her first child, Lyndsey experienced many physical and emotional issues that Western medicine could not explain. It was through human design, Kundalini yoga and homeopathy that she was able to reclaim her wellness again. Armed with these tools, she was able to have her second child in a completely different, very conscious and transcendent experience.

Lyndseyharper.com
www.instagram.com/lyndsey_harper_/

11

MARDALENA DAWN TURPEL

THE BODY REMEMBERS

I learned a little mental trick when I was young and I would bump into something accidentally or kick something hard with my toe. I did this so often that I earned the nickname The Colorado Clutz. I would briefly acknowledge the pain, rub the spot briskly and then erase the memory from existence. Or, so I thought. Inevitably, someone would gasp and point, asking, "Oh my! How did you get that huge bruise?"

Honestly, I wouldn't remember how or when I hurt myself but erasing the memory didn't erase the injury. Even while I didn't want to acknowledge the pain, my body still had the job of healing. The effects of the injury: the broken blood vessels, the changing colors as the body reabsorbs the blood, the lingering pain. Eventually the mark disappeared but my body remembered and tried it's best to heal, with or without my help.

When our energy chose our meat sacks to inhabit, our meat sacks took that job very seriously. They developed a thorough and complicated defense system to not only protect the body, but also our energy. Being ticklish is a line of defense to try to protect a sensitive or vulnerable area of the body, or maybe an area that just isn't used to being touched. Another way the body protects us with its defense systems is by focusing our awareness on a localized area of pain instead of allowing us to feel all our pain, physical or emotional, at once. Imagine, what would that existence look like? Our body, bringing to our attention all of our pain with the intention of encouraging us to heal. It would be overwhelming, and I am grateful for our body's ability to sometimes mask or hide some of our pain to allow us to focus and live our lives. This organic system can and often does backfire. A good example is muscle memory. A muscle's memory receives the nerve signals to relax or engage. But those signals can get crossed and the muscle can think it's relaxed but in reality it is engaged. These might be what we consider tight or strained muscles. Interacting with the muscle can set the memory back correctly.

Another way our body's defense systems can overreact and backfire is in their ability to absorb our emotional trauma and store it in our cells: our nerve cells, our skeletal cells, our muscle cells. They believe this helps us function in our everyday lives and subsequently survive, as survival is very important to our meat sacks. Much like my 'trick' of ignoring and forgetting bruises, this does not help our energy to process and let go. This leads to more pain that can become physical and chronic. We must process our emotional trauma and let it go.

The summer after I graduated highschool and before I could make it to college, I got pregnant. I didn't realize I had gotten pregnant until after I moved into the dorms and began to attend classes. At least, I tried to attend classes while also running to find a bathroom or at least a trashcan to throw up in, and being completely unable to keep my eyes open while studying in the dorm room I shared with two other women who were strangers to me. I finally went to the school clinic and confirmed it. I was confused and torn about what I should do. As a bisexual woman coming of age in the 1990's, highschool was interesting for me to say the least. At one point, a dead fish was left on the hood of my car along with threatening messages written on my window. I had been pining for my life to 'finally begin' with the magical opportunities promised by college life. On the other hand, I really believed I loved the gentleman whose genetics were mixing with mine inside my womb. I also knew that being a mom was meant to be a primary part of my story. My own mother was raised being told the only thing she could be was a wife and mother. Although I know she loved her children, I also know she had other dreams. She raised me fiercely to believe I could be anything and I have carried that with me. Family has always meant so much to me, and the more time I spend moving through this life I have come to realize the gravity of my role in the stories of lineage told and connected through me. I am not a passive rider on this line through the ages and this decision was going to greatly affect my path. I always wanted to be a mother.

After speaking with my partner, we decided together the timing wasn't right and I returned to the student clinic to terminate my pregnancy.

I wasn't ready to let go of that little one's energy yet, so I kept it tied to me. I could see it and feel it, spiraling off my right hip. I didn't share with many people about the pregnancy or abortion and I immediately started to feel my heart tearing from the stress of living a double life. Not being able to grieve publicly, pretending but not being able to experience the 'magical opportunities' promised by college life. I dropped out the next semester.

There was a delicate, twisted comfort in the pain. When I became still, I was able to feel—and sometimes clearly see—the spiral of her energy still attached to me. Nobody else could see or feel her, and very few people even knew about her. She was not coming earthside with me but I still had a connection to her; floating off my right hip, over the front of my pelvis down into my womb.

A few months later, my partner was in a car accident and was in a coma for nine months. This grief combined with my secret grief over the life I ended broke me for a long while. Eventually, I began to open up about the pregnancy and abortion and incorporate them into the line of my life's story. I didn't need to feel the painful, comforting pull of her spiral attached to me as much. During this time, I started massage school and began my healing journey.

Life went on after that, as it does. I graduated school, worked up the courage to start practicing massage and then the courage to work as a massage therapist full time. I worked at a Healing Center then with a Chiropractor, at a Hotel Spa and ended up at a Hair and Spa as the only massage therapist for a while. I got married and became pregnant for the second time. I carried to term and brought our healthy baby boy earthside.

I birthed him in a hospital but as a young, healthy mother with a problem-free pregnancy I was assigned a midwife employed by the hospital instead of an OB-GYN for delivery. She facilitated the most connected experience of my life. After my baby's head emerged, she told me to drop my arms and pull him out of my body myself. Not having worked with a doula or midwife or had any discussions about participating in the birth this way, I instinctively dropped my arms and pulled my baby from my body, bringing him to rest on my breasts. I can only feebly attempt to describe the feeling of pulling him from my body to join us earthside. A flash of pure connection to creation. I felt a similar flash when life started inside of me the first time. I didn't know what the feeling was at the time, and I didn't feel it the three subsequent times I became pregnant but I am certain now that is what I felt.

With my earthside baby, I was having the co-sleeping, breastfeeding, attachment parenting motherhood experience of my dreams! Then I threw my back out for the first time.

As a new mom, my priorities shifted and taking care of myself slipped down the list. After a few days of bedrest, I scheduled a handful of massages for myself and started to feel better. Quickly wanting to forget about this brief, painfully physical interruption, I went back to my peacefully playful mommy life. I equally tried to ignore the nagging pain that had developed in my right hip. Hip problems were common in the women on my mom's side of the family. I don't know how or when exactly, but I subconsciously decided this pain in my hip was just a part of who I was.

After all, I am on the taller side of humans, with really long legs. I was a competitive dancer for years and that is bound to have taken a toll on my body. My mom was always telling me bad hips run in our family. This must just be a natural part of the aging process. It's hell getting old, isn't that what they say? But I was only thirty-one...

Then I threw out my back again.

Lower back pain began to be my specialty massage as the Universe sent me clients with this issue to help teach me to heal myself. Through the door of my life sauntered George: a 78 year old, 6'2" tall silver haired, quick-witted fox with lower back and leg pain. We began working together monthly, then every other week, and soon weekly. We have been working together for twelve years.

Our consistent work together helped me discover the existence of what I call "sister muscles" and the role of the *piriformis* in back pain. When a muscle becomes overextended, there is often a sister muscle that is hyper-constricted. Releasing the hyper-constriction automatically allows the overextended muscle to also have room to relax. Being creatures of habit, the muscles will want to return to that state, so we then need to work with the muscle memory to set the signals from the nervous system straight again. The piriformis is a muscle that connects the big, strapping back and hip muscles to the front groin and inner thigh muscles. Releasing the piriformis is difficult given its location deep in the pelvis, but it holds the anatomical connection between these two sister groups.

With this revelation, I realized where my hip pain was really coming from. It was coming from you, the little spiral of energy attached to my womb. I had forgotten about you. Well, I hadn't forgotten about you exactly, but I didn't realize I had never set you free. Even though I had stopped playing with you and depending on you and I didn't hold you as tightly anymore, I hadn't let you go and my body remembered. I was aware now and ready to do the emotional release work to let you go. I ended up carrying the pain of you with me for over ten years. That duration of suffering leaves some scars and gets intertwined pretty deeply in all aspects of one's mind and body—it isn't something that can be resolved overnight.

My massage practice began to evolve and a magical thing started to happen. A client and I would be working together, and with the release of muscle tension it would come, a beautiful flow of tears. A deep emotional release facilitated by rewiring the neuromuscular response and relieving our meat sack from the burden of tightly held emotions.

Some people recognise the cause right away, as they are conscious of the pain and actively seeking ways to heal. Others are caught off guard by the tears but begin to remember and release. Some people have no idea why they are crying and can often become embarrassed by expressing their emotions. Wherever they are in their journey, we breathe together and I hold space for them. For many, this may be their first step into this beautiful world of self-healing, and I am beyond honored to help them through the portal.

Like any old injury, my hip and lower back will always be a 'weak' spot for me. A chink in the armor where dis-ease can sneak in. I am okay with this. I will need to continue to give extra care and attention to strengthen my beautiful core, to keep myself healthy and moving. One of the many things I learned about aging well from my friend, George, was to acknowledge and support the changes our meat sacks make as they age. Acknowledge, support and change the habits we need to so that we may evolve to the next stage.

Touch is so powerful. Massage can be one of the first steps in your healing journey. Step through the portal and allow yourself to experience the relief, love and gratitude towards this magnificent meat sack, fearlessly carrying your energy through this life!

ABOUT THE AUTHOR

MARDALENA DAWN TURPEL

Mardalena Dawn Turpel is the owner and operator of Mardalena's Massage. Specializing in deep tissue and neuro-muscular emotional release, she is also trained in acupressure, cupping, and Reiki, Swedish, sorts, prenatal massages. Through Mardalena's massage techniques, she works with her clients to bring relief from physical pain and release emotional trauma trapped in the tissues. This is her life's calling and she has been privileged to have spent her time practicing massage since 1999. Mardalena lives in Pleasanton, California with her husband, five boys and their cat, Jaspar.

www.Mardalenadawn.com
www.instagram.com/mardalenasmassage/

12

MARITÈ SALATIELLO

THE DAY I HAD TO GROW UP

Quit or run away?

Two words to describe the story of my life.

Shame and rage the two corresponding feelings.

OCTOBER 2021

I remember my grandfather's apartment. He was seated on his chair in front of a refined Tuscan wood desk with a big view of the city behind him. He was always working, always busy. He used to tell me: "Princess, don't cry. Vulnerability is a liability, and plus you're ugly when you cry".

I was scared of him, but I loved the way he called me princess and how I felt safe in his presence.

I've been spending my life subconsciously avoiding that vulnerability, and avoiding disappointing people like my grandpa.

He was successful, an important entrepreneur in Sicily, strong, and a little crazy.

I wanted to become like him one day: strong, powerful, respected.

OCTOBER 2000

I want to be an actress. Today Mom will drop me to drama class for the first time in my life. I'm excited and so scared. I'm shy, and maybe not able to do any of that.

I don't know what we are going to do. But I'm happy.

I will never go back to drama class again. The teacher humiliated me in front of all the other people. I blushed all over my face and neck like a red balloon and the more I was blushing the more he would make fun of me.

I thought acting would be fun. Instead it was a nightmare being on stage, mocked by him.

Shame all over my body.

SEPTEMBER 7TH 2001

I kissed Fabio tonight, and my heart goes boom! It was the end of summer party at the sea club. He wore a Hawaiian flowers shirt, red New Balance sneakers and a pair of yellow Oakleys. He picked me up with his smurf blue scooter. He's so crazy.

Singular, stylish, charismatic.

Oh my God. I have feelings for him, true beautiful feelings. We kissed in front of the sea over a rock, just the moon and the stars and us. Then he puked but I didn't take it personally. He said that was the best puke of his life.

MARCH 2008

The eight most beautiful years of my life. I'm breaking up with him, I'm moving out of Sicily AND he gives me a handmade painting of his own making?!!

A painting of me on a Sicilian truck, leaving our city, with my dog on the side, and all our places, colors, food, things on the top of the truck.

What kind of man in the world gives a love painting to someone who's running away from him?

I still love him, but I have to go. I have to grow up. I can't live in this bubble forever. I need to expand, to explore—I need to know how the world works.

But his scent, his arms, his hands. Those things...I can never have enough.

APRIL 2009

Fabio came here to Rome. We spent all the time together. We went to Casina Valadier and we had our food ritual. I missed him and our way to honor life. No one knows better than us how to enjoy life. He wrote me a poem and I did the same for him.

We looked at the view of Rome from the Pincio hill, and he said to me: "The world is yours."

DECEMBER 14TH 2012

It's my graduation day. I got my law degree—finally I've made it! I know, it took me three more years than the standard, but I did it! My grandfather *must* be happy for me from heaven.

My parents should be happy too. They always said to me when I told them I wanted to be an actress that first I had to get my degree, and then I could do whatever I wanted.

It's supposed to be a happy day—maybe the happiest of my life. I've finally achieved something so important. But instead, I am sad and feel profoundly empty? I'm scared of what comes next. What will my future hold?

JUNE 2015

I'm sick of all of this, I'm sick of this place, of these people around me, of Rome and all the bullshit that I do. I'm sick of him and all the demands he keeps asking of me. I hope with all my heart that I will not pass the lawyer exam so I can just concentrate on acting.

And I'm so sick of all the promises that I hear. I'm sick of men's repelling attempts to buy me with Rolexes and jewelry. I'm sick of the way they look at me like I am something to eat, or touching me when they get closer, and especially I am sick of myself pretending to be a part of this horrible theatre.

I am sick of thinking that someone else can change my life. I'm sick of this life, these parties, being nice, dressing nicely, speak nicely, smile nicely. I'm NOT fuck'n nice.

I feel lonely, I miss Fabio. Why am I not with him right now? I could have been safe in his arms, loved, and happy.

DECEMBER 2018

Back from New York, I've decided to jump on a last minute plane and come home for holidays.

No family will be here for Christmas but Fabio will.

I'm so excited. I can't wait to show him all of my progress preparing my Barbra Streisand character.

We are going to hide in our bubble and lock ourselves in.

We'll eat, we'll have a bath, and we'll drink the best wine which will reveal our secrets.

I mean I don't reveal *all* of them to him because I'm scared to disappoint him, but he knows me so well that I don't need even to talk.

I will cry and he will hold my tears and kiss them, and then kiss me.

And when the bubble blows up, I will run away.

He will come back to his ordinary life.

We hate ordinary. We belong to each other. We belong to that bubble.

No place for us. No time for us. No past. No future, just the two of us

I love him.

FEBRUARY 2019

So happy I've convinced Fabio to come back to painting!

He got a new canvas and has many ideas washing over him. He has sent me the first photo of his drawing. I love it. It's purple and red, with some stains of yellow that can't be missed.

This is what he needs! And I've also almost convinced him to come here to New York to visit me. Not yet, but close.

And in return, he has inspired me with my Barbra Streisand show. Every Monday we spent hours on the phone to prepare me for the next scene. He wants Barbra to be dressed in this way or that way, he wants her to enter from the window, he thinks she should be pregnant. Endless incredible ideas. We cheer each other up as always.

MARCH 2020

So many things to do. The acting studio is officially closed and I have to move somewhere else because my flatmate is coming back from Los Angeles.

New York is a concentration of COVID-19 and desperation.

Fabio is helping me to find a new place. I will likely move to Albany. I feel safe to be nearer to Governor Cuomo.

I have no intention to give up on the show of Barbra, and no intention to give up on my immigration visa. After all I have done to stay and work here, it is the last thing I want to do.

I need help, I am alone, an immigrant in New York, broke and I have to make all of this possible.

I will. God knows how, but I will.

MAY 2020

Fabio and I are spending entire nights on the phone. Like we always have, but with quarantine it has been crazy! With the different timezone, we start talking at my 6pm and we finish at midnight, which is 6am for him. I always tell him to hang up, but he doesn't want to sleep.

He has this dislike for sleeping. He's always had it since he was nineteen.

He fights it. It's like a competition, and he says that he prefers to live than to sleep.

And I'm no help, because we always have something to say, to share or just to be.

Isn't it crazy that we are so close even when we are physically so far away from each other ?

Tonight, he made me a promise. I asked him: "What if I fail as an actress?

Would you save me? Would you give me food, shelter and love?"

He said, "I will always love you, even if you become homeless. And one day, I will marry you. You will be in your sixties with a grey bob, beautiful as you are now."

JUNE 12, 2020

Today I've shared with Fabio how happy I am to turn thirty-five on June 30, because I feel that there will be a significant change for me. I feel something important is going to happen, and that I've decided to buy myself a tree for my birthday.

Fabio said that it's all coming, just to wait for two more weeks.

He also asked me to let him buy me the tree, an olive tree he said, because it's like me: elegant, strong, and special because it produces such an important thing: the olive oil.

"Your olive oil is your vulnerability. You are the only one who knows who I am because of your heart and empathy. Never lose it, never hide it. It's the reason why I've been loving you for so long. Your heart. Your way to feel. The way you make me feel. Despite your douche face. You are an olive tree."

JUNE 13TH, 2020, 7AM

Went to bed at 3am in the morning and I'm waking up at 7am??

I've got a deep sharp pain in my belly. It's not my stomach, it's not the food. It's something different, like anxiety. I can't breathe.

But I have so many things to do today! I've got the meeting with the production team and I gotta prepare the immigration papers for the lawyer. I have to send the email for the press...but it looks like I'm not going to do any of those things until I understand what is going on here.

The sharp pain is getting stronger.

I'm going to get a coffee and keep writing. I also need to text Fabio about the name of that kind of furniture I had in high school. Yes, I'll text him right now.

JUNE 13, 2020 2PM

While I prepare my favorite meal, ravioli with homemade sauce, I call my sister.

She's tired and upset as usual. I start eating my ravioli. Omg, I love it.

I can see an incoming call from my brother while speaking.

"Mmm, no, I won't get it. I will call him back," I think.

One minute more, and another call comes in but from my dad. "This time I'll get it." Maybe it's something urgent.

While chewing my 3rd raviolo, I answer the call.

Me : "Papa? Is everything all right?"

Papa : "Mari...something bad has happened. I need you to put yourself in a quiet place where eventually you can get help."

My raviolo goes sideways. I start coughing, I feel the blush all over my body, I feel the sharp pain. And I ask my dad to not say another word until I say so.

"No dad, I'm not ready, I'm not ready." Trying to get some breath back in my body.

I open the door window that looks out onto a main street in Albany, with a short intake of breath, I ask him: "Is Martino dead?"

And he said: "No, Fabio is dead."

SEPTEMBER 14TH 2020

Premiere of *The Way I Am*

"Vulnerability, Maritè, find the courage to give your character that level of depth that is in you. You and only you have it. Don't neglect it, go deep and give it to Barbra."

My acting coach's words are on my mind while I am preparing to go on stage. It's the premiere, but my acting coach will not be here, nor my family, nor Fabio.

I'm prepping backstage on the rooftop of a building in Upper East Side, New York, where my team and I have set up a stage due to COVID-19 restrictions to be outdoors, respecting social distancing, and with a limited number of people.

I'm on skates, because that's how Fabio and I wanted Barbra to appear in the first scene.

I look up to the sky and I know he's there with me, and I know he's proud of me. I haven't run away this time, I haven't quit. No shame and no rage are running through my body. Just a sense of deep love for him and for this craft, the craft of acting, the place where I can be the most vulnerable character in the world. The place where I don't have to hide, where I can expose all my weakness, all my pain, all my joy and my craziness. The place where I feel safe within my body and my emotions. The place where I will always bring him with me, in every breath, in every move, in every smile or glance. In every character I play, there will always be a part of him, a part of us. I will make our bubble live on, consistent and unbreakable.

October 2021

I'm writing from my grandpa's chair in Italy. I didn't get the immigration visa, partly because I was working with a horrible lawyer.

After two weeks of *The Way I Am,* I realized that I've picked the wrong people to work with, so now I'm creating a new version of the show.

I need to come back to my roots, to him. I need to process the pain and the truth behind the pain, because the pain is just a key that serves to open a big door. Just like Alice in Wonderland, you have to find the right door.

And on the other side of the door, there's the side of you that you haven't been able to fully love and accept.

He forced me to look at my shadows. He forced me to look at my truth and fears. He forced me to stop the pony show that I've always been so good at.

He forced me to stop doing every single thing that would detract from my authenticity and vulnerability. Stop having men in my life to be saved by or getting help from, stop being the victim, stop hiding, stop being nice, stop not telling my truth.

That day, June 13 2020, was the day I had to grow up.

And I have to say that since then I've been doing the work, the deep work, the shit work, and now I am here and on my grandpa's chair, writing on his refined Tuscan wood desk, and for the very first time in my life, I feel exactly as I dreamed I would feel when I was a little princess: strong, powerful, respected.

Now I am safe.

ABOUT THE AUTHOR

MARITÈ SALATIELLO

Maritè is an actress, theatrical and movie producer, author and coach. She works on the body and the emotions on an artistic and healing level. She has started her personal development journey by studying The Method Acting at the Susan Batson Studio in New York City based on trauma, childhood and emotional body work.

As an artist she thinks that creativity is a huge part of healing and healing is a necessary part of creativity. They must work together.

After graduating from The Integrative Healing School by Jana Alonso, she has put her attention towards Shamanic medicine, the nervous system, trauma release work, embodiment practices and manifestation.

By combining her studying with acting and healing, Maritè has created her own method to work on emotional blockages and embodiment that she teaches in 1on1 or group sessions.

www.maritesalatiello.com
www.instagram.com/i_am_marite/

13

MELISSA LAMBOUR

BEYOND LINEAGE: OUR COSMIC CONNECTION

"You are a global citizen of the world, connecting us back home to the cosmos irregardless of where our roots have been planted. You remind us that we have always belonged, beyond flesh and bone. I'm so excited for others to receive what you have to offer as you map us back to our dharma." - Jumakae

My mentor and past client Jumakae sums up my work so beautifully. She understands what it feels like to live between two worlds, like most children born to immigrant parents. Sense of belonging is a human need that runs deep in every single one of my Astrogeography client sessions. I'm cosmically bonded to Jumakae through my Moon Node line, which runs through Southern Thailand. Harnessing the energy on this astrological line brings me closer to my purpose. It's no surprise that it also runs near my partner's homeland of Malaysia. My connection to that land was fated and written in the stars!

I first met my Malaysian partner, Faris, while playing Dance Dance Revolution as undergrads at Stevens Institute of Technology. We both loved rock music, killer solos and listened to "November Rain" by Guns N' Roses while studying at the library. He always helped me understand engineering principles without undermining my intelligence. He finally won me over with food, which he still does to this day. Our cross-cultural connection sparked my travel bug, and we began traveling very early in our relationship. We traveled to my parents' homeland, Guatemala, to experience the colonial cities, villages, volcanoes, lakes and the ancient Mayan ruins of Tikal. Faris was a keeper, since he loved street food as much as me! Our next trip was back to his homeland, where I got to experience the warmth of his culture and the food. When his student visa expired, it was time for him to move back to Malaysia. We didn't want to marry just for the sake of getting his green card, so we chose to see how things would go as a long-distance relationship. It was the best decision we ever made since it allowed us to meet in Europe and Asia during those three years.

ASIA WAS WAITING FOR ME WITH OPEN ARMS (AND FOOD)!

I've been to Malaysia almost a dozen times, sometimes against Faris' will, but I feel so loved and cared for there. I didn't know back then, but I was tapping into planetary energies that only Astrogeography could explain.

Mama Azizah

A frail, Muslim woman showed me what unconditional love truly was. Mama Azizah was the grandmother I wish I had.

Even as a mat salleh, *a foreigner,*
She welcomed me into her traditional house in the Kampung, *the village.*
The simplicity and richness of the culture had me coming back for more.
The land of dragon fruit, mangosteen, sweet fuzzy rambutan and the
unmistakable durian.
Why did I feel so at home there?
It wasn't even my blood lineage!
It was my chosen lineage or the lineage that chose me,
That I was destined to dance with in this lifetime.
I'm meant to work with the spirit of my chosen ancestors and the energies
of the land,
So I may understand the true meaning of bridging cultures.
Do you ever meet people and wonder why you're so drawn to them?
They may carry or embody the planetary energies you were destined to
connect with.
Malaysia is my home, my mother, my grandmother,
Welcoming me back every time with open arms and food.
"Dah Makan?" "Have you eaten?"

Guatemala is a neutral zone for me on my astromaps, but Southeast Asia, Hong Kong, and China have major energies related to my home, family, purpose, healing and transformation. I now understand that you can connect to these planetary energies through people, culture, practices, and objects. Even meditating on these things can allow you to harness the energy of a place. My favorite way to harness the energy of Malaysia is by wearing flowy traditional batik kaftans that caress my skin. I channel every artisan that crafted these textiles. I embody *Makcik* energy all the way by enjoying the simplicity of life (pronounced "Mak-cheek", Malay for Auntie). I miss going to the *mamak* food stalls, the bustling markets, and hanging out, or *lepaking* as the locals call it, until the wee hours of the night. I was blessed with very chill in-laws that took me in, even when I was just dating their son. If seen through the conservative Islamic lens of Malaysia, our relationship could have been problematic and frowned upon. I stuck out like a sore thumb in Southeast Asia, but everyone's curiosity and generosity was endearing.

We tend to think that we must be loyal only to our ancestral bonds. But what if they are severed physically or emotionally due to years of pain and generational trauma? When my parents divorced, my paternal family ties were never the same again. The road trips I had loved to plan to Florida became a thing of the past. At sixteen, around the same time my dad last spoke to me as a teenager, I convinced my mom to take me and my sister to the bus stop in Atlantic City so that the two of us could take the bus down to Fort Lauderdale. Even back then, nobody could say "no" to my crazy ideas. I wanted to be down in Florida with my father's family, even if my father wasn't around. They were my lifeline and direct access to my cultural identity. Up in New Jersey, I didn't know what Guatemalan culture was outside of making tamales for Christmas and extravagant Sweet 16 parties that felt more like traditional Quinceañeras. My Latinness was pieced together from all the other cultures I grew up with in the Spanish-speaking Catholic Church. We'd get authentic Mexican tamales and tacos from downtown Lakewood. I appreciated my multicultural upbringing and the way the Spanish language opened my world beyond New Jersey. I learned the nuances of every country, the way they spoke, and what they ate. I may not have been fully immersed in Guatemalan culture, but I was swimming in a rich *caldo* of Latinness.

Being raised on Lenape land with no direct lineage to my ancestors made reclaiming my Indigenous roots difficult. I was also called to other parts of the world, where there are planetary energies I was meant to connect with based on Astrogeography. I know that with every generation, my ancestors lost touch with their Indigenous roots due to colonization as they delved deeper into Catholicism and further away from their ancient practices. Astrogeography connects me back to my ancestors that looked to the stars and planets for answers. I reclaim my ancestral connection to the cosmos and divination. I wish to bring Astrogeography into the light, so I can develop "Cosmic Roadmaps" for people worldwide. As I travel the world and work with Astrogeography to bridge unlikely cultures, I heal my lineage. We no longer have to make decisions from a place of desperation; we have the choice to heal through our passions. I carry the torch to guide you back to the cosmos and find true belonging.

WHO AM I TRULY?

I was cracked open when I was told to leave an online BIPOC space. I had flown into this global community like a moth to a flame, only to be burned by the most unexpected encounter. It was a Queer, sex-positive, BIPOC-friendly community that was meant to be a safe space. With the Black Lives Matter movement at its peak, BIPOC spaces began springing up. Was I welcomed in these spaces? Like most Latin American families, mine was every imaginable shade of brown and beige. After months of trying to figure out the right words to describe myself, I settled on "white Latina". I was immediately told to leave the space since it was only meant for Black, Indigenous, and People of Color. This was a space that I thought I rightfully belonged in because of my lived experience, not necessarily the color or shade of my skin. After further explaining that I was white-presenting and light-skinned, but of Guatemalan descent, there was more understanding. Now looking back, I could have left out the word "white" like I had done most of my life, but it was such a polarizing time, that it felt necessary to take a side, either White or Black, without an in-between. I didn't know how I fit into a BIPOC space. Was I a white-presenting POC with Afro-Indigenous roots? As someone of mixed ancestry, I was ethnically ambiguous and often perceived as "white" until I opened my mouth or hit the dance floor. This was a form of reverse racism and colorism that I never expected to confront, but knew that moving forward I wanted to create spaces that understood the nuances of ethnicity and culture. I appreciated the Asian people that reached out to check on me during this mishap since they somehow understood where I was coming from. We don't always fit the stereotypes, nor should we. Only we have a say who we are and how we identify.

***

My ancestors are from the land of volcanoes,
lush mountains, mystical lakes and ancient ruins,
where the rhythmic sounds of the marimba wake up the soul,
and the corn feeds it.
Where the stories of my ancestors are woven
and embroidered into bright rainbow masterpieces,
but have been erased from my lineage due to colonization.
They were people of the land and of the cosmos,
observers, inventors, nomads, traders, healers...

***

Growing up, being called "white" or "blanquita" always rubbed me the wrong way. It completely dismissed my culture and the struggles my parents had to endure to set up their life in the US after leaving Guatemala. However, I now acknowledge my white-presenting privilege and have had deep conversations with Faris about how we are both seen differently in this world. I know that I will always be given preferential treatment for my lighter skin and features. It's something that I must accept and use for good by continuing to be a bridge in BIPOC conversations. No matter how I'm perceived, the struggles are universal in our diverse BIPOC/immigrant communities, especially the issue of absent fathers. The reality is that my deep father wound continues to rear its ugly head. Whether it was unrequited love or being told to leave a BIPOC space, those events opened an even deeper abandonment wound that I had been carrying since I was 16 years old. Why have I felt like I don't belong in this world? Maybe because I had been carrying around this false idea that my father never wanted me, so the rest of the world wouldn't either.

The months that followed were filled with journaling, heavy feelings of not belonging, and searching for the proper words to describe my existence. I stumbled upon an Oracular Leadership Summit that showcased primarily BIPOC healers and coaches. I instantly connected to Jumakae's story as a Thai-American that yearned to connect back to her ancestral land, only to find out that her Story Medicine business was meant to be birthed back at home in Southern California. We finally connected through one of her Story Medicine workshops, which allowed me to start healing what had happened earlier that year. I was hesitant to take up space, still traumatized that I'd be called out for being "white" and told to leave.

The truth was that I felt more Malaysian than Guatemalan after having been with my partner for over sixteen years, the same amount of time I spent with my father as a child. My taste in food, music and entertainment had expanded. It's cliche, but Faris definitely stole my heart through my stomach! He was a foodie just like me, where flavor and spice were top priority. We both devoured Anthony Bourdain's shows after college. We couldn't get enough of him and other food vloggers on Youtube. They opened our eyes to the world through food, and Bourdain's love affair with Asia paralleled my own. I would eventually travel to Malaysia and Vietnam just like he did to experience it myself.

In 2018, the whole world, especially Faris and I, mourned Anthony Bourdain. He was the father figure I never had. My Facebook post two days after Bourdain passed reads *JUN 10, 2018:*

RIP. I'm still processing it all, it's just so surreal. I learned from his travels that food has the power to bring diverse groups of people to the table. May we continue in his legacy and try to have deeper, more honest conversations that will hopefully bring about change.

I was inspired to continue his legacy of bridging cultures through food and travel. In 2019, I silently grieved my cousin, who also took her life and left behind a family and children that loved her. Their deaths made me rethink the trajectory of my life, and to stop coasting along without a purpose. I quickly dove into living my most authentic self and finally traveling solo around South America and Southeast Asia. In April 2019, I even had the chance to eat at the same restaurant that Obama and Bourdain had their famous meal back in 2016. It was a full circle moment. From that point on, I knew I had to travel with purpose; no more searching aimlessly like I had in the past, jumping from one dopamine hit to another. I was done filling the emptiness with experiences only to be left in a dark, lonely hotel room. As a traveler, I knew I had to befriend my inner world before I tried to escape somewhere else in my outer world. My partner always kept me grounded. He knew what I stood for and respected me for always being open to different cultures—not just the flavor of the day, but the way I fully immersed myself in the nuances and contradictions.

DEATH AND REBIRTH: SHEDDING IDENTITIES

With death comes rebirth. 2018 marked the beginning of a new Melissa, while in 2019 I searched for my purpose. Losing Bourdain and my cousin brought things into perspective. It was my turn to live the life of my dreams, not one that I was expected to follow. My business was birthed at the very moment my identity was completely shattered. Talk about death and rebirth! I was left to pick up the pieces for the rest of the year. I was robbed of my voice, which led me to Egypt to try to heal my throat chakra. 2021 was a devastating inner battle of figuring out what spaces accepted me or not, and being honest about the spaces I wanted to cultivate moving forward. And 2022 will be the year I reclaim all my ancestral wisdom and traditions across the globe. I stand strong as the person I've become against all odds and obstacles. I lean into my medicine without fear of persecution. I feel like I'm constantly shedding identities and roles in order to start anew. I touch upon this concept in my *Legacy Speaks* chapter, "Beyond Labels: Finding your place in the World." I honor my ancestral lineage from Guatemala and welcome my chosen family from Malaysia. I am the bridge, meant to connect Guatemala to Malaysia. An unlikely pair that I love to call "Guatelaysia".

GUIDING YOU BACK TO THE COSMOS: BELONGING

We often think we're stuck or can't change our situation, but the truth is Astrogeography can show you the way and explain why you've felt disconnected or drawn to travel the world in search of your "home". Finding home beyond your ancestry, especially when you feel called elsewhere. My vision is to bridge cultures and connect people with harmonious energies, regardless of their background or labels. I'm here to guide you back to your cosmic family, the home you never knew existed. Astrogeography will explain why you have cosmic connections around the world with the most unexpected people, cultures and places. You'll finally align with the planetary energies that you were destined to connect with in this lifetime since it *was* written in the stars!

My legacy is to help YOU stop escaping yourself and find peace right where you are.

I do this work for every person that has ever felt like an outsider. Every person deserves a place to call home, whether it's on this earth or within their soul. Allowing your inner and outer world to reach an equilibrium.

As I begin tapping into my unique planetary energies around the world, I realize that some places will bring me to my shadows, while others will bring me to my light. Egypt most recently brought me to the depths of my soul. This poem was born on a sailboat in the middle of the Egyptian Red

Sea as I tapped into the cosmic energies of the dolphins (descendants of the star, Sirius B) as well as spiritual Neptune, transformational Pluto and healing Chiron from my astromaps. At that moment, I was actually homesick for Malaysia, not the US. I surely was craving my moon node energy to bring me back to my purpose. I dedicate this to the runner within me and all the endless wanderers that wish to find their cosmic connection.

The Runner
She stares into the golden sun,
Wondering where the fun has gone?
How did she get here?
She feels the waves up against the boat,
Swaying it back and forth.
As she wonders about her worth,
She wonders if she deserves this life?
Is she dreaming,
Or living this in real life?
She wishes to be free,
So she can see,
What this world is meant to be?
Is she running away, or
Running towards her fate?
Like a fish in the sea,
Drawn to the bait,
She gets lured to the wonders of the world.
Her adventure has just begun,
She can't fathom it ever being done!

ABOUT THE AUTHOR

MELISSA LAMBOUR

Melissa Lambour is a spiritual globetrotter that turned her wanderlust into her life's work when she became a Reiki AstroGeo Guide and founded Cosmic Roadmap. She guides the endless wanderer to discover their place in the world with her signature Astrogeography sessions! Weaving together Reiki, Ayurveda and Astrogeography, she has helped digital nomads and avid travelers develop a Cosmic Roadmap that determines their next steps in life and business. She strives to serve people from all walks of life, especially individuals belonging to the 2SLGBTQIA+, BIPOC and immigrant communities that have felt out of place or called to travel the world. In addition to being a digital nomad, she holds a BE/ME in Mechanical/Biomedical Engineering and an MBA in Sustainability Management with twelve years of career experience. With twenty countries under her belt, she plans to "astromap" her way around the world using Astrogeography to experience all of her best planetary energies.

linktr.ee/MELISSALAMBOURLLC

14

MELISSA RUIZ

PROTECT

*W*hen I think of lineage, nothing good immediately comes to mind. As a Puerto Rican and first generation born in the States and not on the island, the first flashes that come into my head are Taino Indians enslaved by the Spanish. Lineage = rape and pillage. Awesome. My dark-skinned grandfather had blue rings around his deep brown eyes. My light-skinned mother passed as white. And she informs so much of who I interpret myself to be. She was my first mirror in life. And I never quite knew what I was looking at when I looked at her. She was "mom". She was the boss. She was always right.

But I don't naturally raise my left eyebrow when I am being sassy because of her. How many past generations of current Melissa particles did that? How many women felt lost and found at the same time like I do now? How many generations felt here and there at the same time? What a cool thing to consider. It's less lonely to think that someone, somewhere in time, created a ripple effect for me to be here as I am in all my glory.

Rumor has it that the female line of my family on my mom's side is cursed. Something about a lover that was jealous of my mom. While it could explain a lot of the "WTF" moments in life, I also think life is one big confusing mess of decisions we try to explain away. Taking a chance by writing this chapter is downright frightening. It feels like I am betraying an unwritten rule of silence passed on to me. I struggle with this for a few reasons: 1. I was told not to air out our dirty laundry because it's no one else's business. This included therapy. I went on to get my Master's in Social Work. "Be a therapist, but don't go to therapy. Check! 2. Suffering is universal, but while growing up it felt like only my mom could suffer. I was never shown what pain, reconciliation, or even authentic joy looked like, so when tasked to create it or share, I struggle. 3. When I gave a TEDx talk a couple years ago, I could not find the right way to speak about my experience without speaking about my mom. I wanted to protect her. I didn't want to speak badly about her, or have her hear that I was talking about my experiences growing up. It's all connected though. Her actions or words that led to my pain then—and my learning now— are all connected in this web of human development and connection. I didn't have access to that interpretation growing up, so it felt easy to look for someone to blame. I am sharing this now, and in this format, because I now see that without certain people saying certain things at certain times, my entire life could be completely different.

The word protection comes to mind when I think of my lineage. It is much deeper than people I look like or sound like; it is people that now protect me on my path in this world. I often find myself asking family members for help. Let me be clearer: I ask the dead ones. My mother was a single mom and, while I know my father, I don't *know* my father. As a matter of fact, I don't *know* my mother either. She ruled the house and I don't remember much of what I did or said that made her smile. There was usually a Puerto Rican hip pop, an eye roll and smirk that displayed her disappointment. We don't speak, though not for lack of me trying.

I started saying that I don't think my mom knows how to be a mother to adult children. The older I got, the less of a chance I gave her to try. When she definitively detached emotionally from me, I stopped trying. It felt like a release but also a huge disappointment. Another out, another hole, another absence. I see women who like to hang out with their mothers where they ask deep questions, know about family history, and where they got their middle name. I applaud you and I am a little jealous. Mother's Day is triggering. National Daughter's Day is triggering. As a physically grown adult, there are moments when I feel like I am still waiting to cross into adulthood.

I made a decision a while back to exclude toxic people from my life. People that live in the past, people who dwell on things instead of looking for a way to grow, people who looked down on creative expression and relied on routine to get through life all needed less access to me. So, we see each other at weddings and funerals. There are so many more funerals nowadays. The adage is right. The older you get the older everyone gets. And so, when I need help or guidance, I ask the dead. I'm not asking for money or a place to stay. I am asking for the thought, the gut reaction, the right person to say the right thing, or my own ability to notice what I need to notice.

Sometimes this help comes through a feeling. Other times, it's a thought. The most bizarre will come in a premonition of what could be, along with an understanding that I can make choices to get to a different result. It's become more prominent as I have gotten older. I will lean in and tell someone, "I know something isn't right. Let's step aside if you want to talk about it." And they tear up or go for the hug simply for having someone really see them in that moment. I am ignorant about this gift of mine. I can't call it anything but instinct. And I can't even use it when I want to. I think it just happens when I am supposed to help someone, to protect them. When I do, the energy shifts as space is created for healing. My conclusion is that it's women of my past waiting patiently to listen. That's what it feels like. Just listening. That is my only job.

Lineage is about reflection and asking questions that don't make sense to get to the bottom of a feeling you can't shake. Lineage, to me, is curiously embracing the mess of what humans have created. One reflection led me to loss.

My mother and I were at a wedding for a friend from my dance team. When they announced the grandparents of the bride, I leaned over to my mom and said, "I won't have my grandparents at my wedding." My mom was thirty-eight when she had me. My grandparents were already old. At that moment, I saw something come over her. Not quite the regret of getting pregnant; it had been the 80s and it was "impossible to be pregnant at thirty-eight." It was more like recognition and sadness, acknowledging what will be without any way to avoid it. Aside from funerals, it's the last memory I have of her truly emoting.

And still, the word *protection* comes to mind. When I zoom in on my direct experience as a living being, it is full of signals that guide me on a path that is safe. Yes, I have free will and can decide to go any way I want, but I have always felt nudged in certain directions. This nudge also makes it hard for me to be 100% committed to any moment or decision. It seems so transient and disconnected when I look back, but so real and purposeful in the moment. I started looking for an apartment because of a feeling that my partner was going to break up with me, I anticipated losing my job, I dreamed about life in a new city—and it all happened. Some call it living in worry. It's my protection. My guides are telling me to get used to this new idea or new person. "The world is changing; let this unknown be familiar to you," they say. It's like having answers to a test with no questions.

But growing up, life was really confusing growing up without these realizations and interpretations of what was going on. There was a double standard growing up. My mom told my brother that she would rather buy him condoms than diapers. But she told me, "If you want to go on the pill, I will give you one pill. Hold it between your legs until you're thirty." I'll be the first to say, this is hilarious and a line I use in jest to this day. But when you hear it over and over again, it sends you messages. She was telling me what I could not do with my body without really telling what I could not do with my body. Looking back, I would have much rather had a conversation with my mom about relationships and intimacy. Instead, I received rules wrapped in sarcasm.

It's not her fault. She did her best and I know that. And I can't help but wonder what messages she received. What was she told that informed how she thought about herself? What messages did she imply based on information presented? How did she feel when her brothers received messages that empowered them and diminished her?

You know those happy, matching outfit family pics on the beach, with everyone in jeans and white t-shirts? It is completely ridiculous to me that people would 1. Pose for those pictures, 2. Frame them, 3. Put them on display. Growing up, we didn't do that. We didn't have school pictures or prom photos lining the staircase like other houses did. No proof that people lived there. Loved there. We had random magnets that covered the refrigerator door, and we decorated with the homemade ceramic party favors you get from people's baby showers and weddings. It was the 90's and it was a weird trend, okay?! Once a week, we'd clean the house and I would find myself dusting so and so's party favor from years before. It seems odd to me now.

Fact: women are superheroes. While my mom was at work, I was looked after by my a rotation of grandmothers on both sides and a bonus "grandmom" that was the grandmother of a cousin. The family tree gets messy here, but it really is where women step up and create the village we so often reference. My mom's mom, "Gram", was particularly present. We would have sleepovers at her apartment, and I can still remember the Lipton's chicken noodle soup and grilled cheese sandwich combo we would have for lunch as we watched *The Price is Right* and the news. She would sleep over at our house during the holidays, and it felt like having a best friend over. I wasn't allowed to spend the night when I was invited to sleepovers. My mom would pick me up really late at night and then bring me back to whoever's house it was early in the morning. It was embarrassing and I hated it. So having sleepovers with Gram felt special and rare. I remember one spring. We came back from a week away for one of my dance competitions and something wasn't quite right with Gram. There was barely any food in her apartment. She looked exhausted and couldn't quite recall how she spent her time while we were away. It's a bit of a blur, but it all became clear with an overwhelming ache and one simple, devastating word: Alzheimer's. I was eleven years old and I grew up fast after that diagnosis. Gram moved in with my mom and I immediately, and my role as granddaughter quickly shifted to caretaker. From gentle reminders and practice reading a calendar to feeding Gram through a feeding tube and rotating her when she could no longer walk, I saw her die slowly every day for seven years. In the middle, where she was vocal but still lost, she would gaze off, eyes fixated on something no one else could see. She would nod her head and shake her hands, sometimes in conversation and sometimes in frustration. I don't think she was alone in those moments. I think she was visited, comforted and maybe even confronted by women from her past as she navigated the disease with fewer and fewer words.

I have learned so much in my reflection of my time with Gram and that disease. As an adult, I see more and I am open to more understanding of my past than I had access to as a child and young adult. I so wish I was wiser then, more present to truly absorb the sacred loss of memories my grandmother was experiencing. While I like to think my empath abilities were developing and I did feel her pain sometimes, the distractions of young adulthood kept me from embracing what was happening around me.

Mom changed in the time Gram was sick. I can't quite pinpoint it. It could have been Gram's Alzheimer's, a midlife crisis, a mental illness she was too proud to get help for. I have no idea. But the mom who took us on vacations and explored new towns when we were away for dance competitions and went on roller coasters with me...was gone. I think I lost my mother in those years. Alzheimer's took two people from me, and I don't know if I'll ever get over that.

I used to say that I would never raise my kids the way my mother raised me. I can't say that anymore. When I open my mouth, my mom comes out! There is no stopping her presence in how I live. And I see the ripple effect of Gram on her, and her mother before that, and on and on. My mother gave me great tools and lessons. But she didn't make them up. She learned them, experienced them first-hand and gave me what she understood from them. In my work as a public speaker and coach, it is my true north to help people be their truest self. For a long time, I was taught to hide, to be quiet, to make life easy for everyone else. Lately, I have only been finding reasons to live out loud, with lots of mistakes, new adventures, tons of charges to my credit card and unlimited sass. My lineage did not suffer for me to play it small or safe. They protect me with every step, and they let me stumble when I need a wake-up call.

Lineage is deeper than who we came from. It is wrapped in the trauma and baggage of everyone before us. In her attempt to protect me, my mother helped me realize that I would rather be met with curiosity and conversation than rules and demands.

Everything we do, see, taste, smell is because of a decision someone made years before we existed. What a scary place to live - in pure potential and hope. It is my hope that we all use that opportunity to recognize and give action to our passed on potential. With every birth, there are expectations and visions for the future. "What could that child do?" "Who will this child be?" "How will that child act?" We get stuck in the *doing* of humanity instead of the *being*. With age comes wisdom, so I am now wondering why I spent so much time doing instead of being, and discovering the amazing, weird, silly human I am today. And I would be none of it without my lineage. There are so many questions and doubts, dreams and decisions I now know had nothing to do with me. They were lined up long before I had a pulse. I can't wait to see how it continues to unfold around me.

ABOUT THE AUTHOR

MELISSA RUIZ

Melissa Ruiz MSW, is a Speaker, Public Speaking Coach and is no stranger to the stage. From community theatre and competitive dance to first runner-up at Miss New Jersey and the TEDx stage, Melissa knows the value of connecting with an audience. She holds her Masters in Social Work from Rutgers University and worked in higher education for almost ten years before transitioning to public speaking. Today she helps leaders in their field overcome their fear of public speaking to create a bigger impact through her signature online course, *Show and Tell with Mel*. She lives in New York City and loves pizza and her 95-pound dog, Gus.

themelissaruiz.com
www.instagram.com/melissa.a.ruiz/

15
MIAUWLING OEI

WITH LOVE & GRATITUDE—HEALING ABANDONMENT AND RECLAMATION OF SELF

*I*t was my first week of fourth grade. I was delighted to be in the courtyard at recess on a sunny autumn day. I closed my eyes and tilted my face to the sky. The sun on my face felt wonderful. Then I heard it. It was loud and disruptive. "Meeeooowww! Meeeooowww! Meeeooowww!" My eyes flung open. I saw large faces inches away from mine screaming that terrible sound. I took several steps back and stared at these faces as they continued to scream "Meeeooowww, meeeooowww, meeeooowww." I stood there paralyzed with a feeling of shame, embarrassment and eventually anger swept over me. Why did I have to be stuck with a name that's ridiculously stupid-sounding? Nobody seems to be able to pronounce it correctly! Finally, in what seems like forever, they turned around, giggling as they walked away.

I was sick and tired of being made fun of by my classmates and feeling embarrassed every day during roll call. Names are listed in alphabetical order, so I knew exactly when my turn came. As if on cue, my teacher would have a painful expression on her face as she tried to pronounce my name. Before she uttered a word, I raised my hand to let her know I'm in the room. Every day, I would go through the same experience. I was too embarrassed to let my teacher know how to correctly pronounce my name.

One afternoon, I came home determined to select a normal name that everyone can pronounce. I was watching a cartoon show called *Alvin & The Chipmunk*. One of the characters on the show is Brittany. In that moment, I decided to adopt the name Brittany. The name sounds pretty, easy to pronounce and very American. I felt excited to attend school the next day. I couldn't wait to tell my teacher my new name. Finally, I was going to be normal. I was going to be just like everyone else.

Before morning roll call, I marched to my teacher feeling proud and happy. I could feel that my life was about to change. I told my teacher to greet me as Brittany instead of Miauwling. It took some time for me to respond when someone called me Brittany, but from that day on, nobody made fun of my name.

In the years that followed, I became accustomed to being called Brittany. I sharpened my skills to be well-liked by others. By the time I was in my twenties, I was very proficient in fulfilling what others needed so that they would be pleased with me. I spent hours on the phone with friends who needed to complain about their problems. Many times, I was the designated driver to take friends home after a night of partying. There was one time when I drove through all five boroughs taking friends home. The sun was just coming up as I reached my front door. I was ready to drop. Friends I had at the time would describe me as nice and dependable. Everyone liked me, yet I didn't feel good about myself. Something didn't make sense to me. I felt invisible. I felt small. I felt unworthy. I felt I didn't matter. I felt that I didn't exist.

To further validate this feeling, I remember an experience while I was in college. It was one of my friend's birthdays. We got two birthday cakes because a large group was gathering to celebrate. I was about to take a bite of cake when I noticed someone without cake. I handed my plate to her thinking I'll just get another one. I looked around and noticed by this time, everyone was already eating. I sat there looking at everyone eating cake. I was the only person without cake. I waited, hoping someone would notice and share their piece of cake with me. Nobody noticed. I fought back tears as I sat there feeling invisible.

It wasn't until years later when I realized I was responsible for this experience and all other experiences where I felt invisible, unworthy and small. It took what felt like an earthquake shaking in my soul for me to understand how things are happening through me instead of to me. I became aware of subtle ways I behaved that perpetuated the beliefs I had about myself.

On January 13, 2012, I was headed home after working a twenty-seven-hour shift as a paralegal at a corporate law firm. Papers from motion for summary judgment were filed and the deadline was met. I could go home. My body was beyond exhaustion. I felt numb as I got into my car. I drove onto the busy streets of midtown Manhattan and instantly burst into tears. I felt the pain from years of feeling invisible, unworthy and small. I started screaming, "Stop! stop! stop!" because the pain I felt was unbearable. I ached in places I didn't know I had inside me. I was willing to do anything to relieve myself from this agony. I looked for a spot to crash my car. I decided to end my life. It was the only solution I could think of in that moment.

I envisioned my funeral. Would anyone notice I was gone? Would people miss me? Would anybody cry? It was in that moment when something struck me. I remembered attending a funeral of a dear friend who took her own life nearly ten years ago. I felt angry and confused that she left everyone who loved her. I also remember whispering to her at the wake that there's another way. This realization was enough for me to make it home safely. That was the day I forgave and accepted my friend's death. I promised myself to find another way.

A week later, I visited my dear friend at the cemetery. The last time I saw her was during her funeral, a decade ago. Once I arrived at the cemetery, I remembered her resting spot as if her funeral was yesterday. I sat next to her feeling oddly relaxed. I asked her to send me strength and guidance. Before long, I would meet people with the same name as my dear friend. They shared stories and messages with me that helped me gain clarity about things in my life.

Months later, Kundalini yoga found me. The practice helped me develop a healthy sense of awareness. I also took up dancing that further helped me work through my sense of self. During dance, I could feel my body merge with the beat and rhythm of the music. It released a range of emotions that helped me feel satisfied and satiated afterward. For several years, my daily after-work activity alternated between kundalini yoga and dancing. Eventually, I became happier. My outlook on life and what I thought about myself became more positive. This was my therapy.

My awareness helped me process what had happened on that fateful day in January. I realized I had steadily slid into a state of depression. I had no idea I was depressed. The earth shattering moment I experienced can be described as hitting rock bottom. I'm deeply grateful to gain this insight about myself.

In September 2016, my birthday gift to myself was a divinely guided Abraham Hicks Law of Attraction workshop offered on a cruise. It was a Mediterranean cruise for twelve nights. Little did I know at the time that my experiences on this trip would come to have a profound impact in the way I thought about myself.

It all started one winter afternoon months earlier. I was listening to a lecture from Wayne Dyer on Youtube. I love his teachings. The Youtube autoplay feature was turned on so another lecture soon followed. I found myself nodding and resonating with the speaker. The topic was about how our thoughts can greatly affect the way we behave from Abraham Hicks Publications. I felt drawn to look them up since I'm not familiar with the teachings of Abraham Hicks. I quickly pulled up their website. I saw a workshop being offered later that year on a Mediterranean cruise for twelve nights. My body perked up as if someone had "dinged" me. I was excited and bewildered at the same time. I heard my inner voice say, "Book it!" So I did.

During my trip, the name "Brittany Oei" was printed on the name tag to be worn at the workshop. The name "Miauwling Oei" was printed on the key card to my room because Miauwling Oei is my official name. It's the name that's on my passport and driver's license. I carried both items every day without the slightest awareness of the lack of integrity in the way I was showing up.

On the seventh day, we were in Gibraltar, UK. I was on my way to the Upper Rock Nature Reserve when I saw a woman with beautiful large eyes. I noticed we were both carrying the same Abraham Hicks tote bag. We smiled, knowing we were both from the cruise. She introduced herself and proceeded to ask me for my name. "Brittany Oei," I said. She looked at me and shakes her head. "What's your real name," she asked? I stared at her. A feeling of guilt and shame swept over me. I was caught red-handed. There was a sense of dread as I remembered unpleasant experiences regarding my name from grade school. With shaky hands, I took out the key card to my room and pointed to my name. Feeling embarrassed, I whispered the name I was given at birth. To my surprise, she smiled and said, "That's a beautiful name and it suits you."

That evening, I wound up at the same dinner table as the woman with beautiful large eyes. She proceeded to introduce me as Miauwling to everyone at the table. I was horrified! I felt sick as memories of my classmates making fun of my name came to mind. I could hear them exaggerating the first word to my name. "Meeeooowww! Meeeooowww! Meeeooowww!" Just when I was about to get up and leave the table, I saw smiling faces looking at me. Eight people sat at the table and each of them greeted me warmly and pronounced my name beautifully.

For decades, my family were the only people who called me Miauwling. Everyone else called me Brittany. To have people I just met greet me as Miauwling was quite an experience. I could feel my body and soul respond deliciously to the sound of my name. Then out of nowhere, I heard it. "Meow meow!" Startled, I turned to look where the sound came from. It was from the woman with those beautiful large eyes. Then others started to join in with the sound. "Meow meow!" I smiled and began to laugh. I noticed they were not making fun of me. Actually, it was endearing. For the remainder of the cruise, I introduced myself as Miauwling. I felt nostalgic, almost like a remembering of something, however I can't put my finger on it.

A few people and I moved to the lounge area after dinner. We fell into a discussion about adopting a nickname when living in a foreign country. I shared with them how I came to adopt the name Brittany. One woman said, my dear, your name given at birth is part of your lineage. I realized my name is my identity and something to be cherished. By adopting Brittany, I had unintentionally disowned myself. It occurred to me that this was the reason why I had been feeling invisible, unworthy and small. Before I went to bed, I wrote in my journal new perspectives and insights I received that day.

The first week I returned to the States, I entertained the idea of instructing everyone to call me Miauwling. That week came and went. I did nothing. I said nothing. Eventually the hustle and bustle of life in New York City took over.

In September 2017, my birthday gift to myself was yet another Abraham Hicks Law of Attraction workshop offered on a cruise. This time, it was a French Riviera cruise for ten nights. Once again, the name "Brittany Oei" was printed on the name tag to be worn during the workshop and the name "Miauwling Oei" was printed on the key card to my room. Once again, I carried both items every day however this time I felt uncomfortable for being a liar.

The first full day on the cruise, I treated myself to quiet time at the spa. I was relaxing in the steam room when I heard a sound that was playful and familiar. "Meow meow!" I smiled and knew exactly who it was. I searched through the steamy room and saw the woman with those beautiful large eyes. I was delighted to see her again.

By this time, I was no stranger to the teachings of Abraham Hicks. The synchronicity of meeting this woman again was a reminder that I have unfinished business with myself. Ever since I experienced being greeted as Miauwling by others, I had been steadily feeling disconnected to the name Brittany. I yearned to hear the sound Miauwling to be spoken from others when they call out to me. Not instructing others to greet me as Miauwling was beginning to feel more painful than the thought of people struggling to pronounce my name correctly, or the thought of someone making fun of my name.

I felt uneasy during the trip. I met wonderful people, visited beautiful places, ate delicious food and had plenty of good laughs, however I could not shake the anxious and unsettled feeling that began to intensify the closer I got to the end of the trip. So, I did what I knew I needed to do. Two days before the completion of the cruise, I carved out quiet time. That evening, I ate dinner alone. I found a spot on the top deck to enjoy my plate of food and appreciate the gorgeous sunset. I was mesmerized by the soft glow of yellow, orange, red, pink and purple all merging together as the sun began to set below the horizon. The sight was breathtaking.

The sight of the vast ocean helped me feel expansive. I felt tears flowing down my cheek and a release of fear that I had held for so long. It no longer mattered who can or cannot pronounce my name.

It no longer mattered who thought my name was weird or made fun of it. None of that mattered anymore. Then I spoke these words: "Goodbye Brittany. Hello Miauwling." That was the moment I came home to me and I felt absolute bliss. I started to laugh and sing parts of the opening song from the workshop. "Joy! Joy! Joy! Joy is the key! I can do it!" I ran downstairs and excitedly shared the good news with friends I made on the ship. I felt victorious to reclaim myself in this way.

Back in the States, I shared with my parents my decision to release the nickname Brittany. I could tell my parents appreciated my decision. They shared that Miauwling means forever young. What a beautiful meaning to my name! That was the day I vowed to never abandon myself ever again. I vowed to cherish me.

Four years later, I am on my laptop stringing words together to share this story. They say there's healing that happens when someone shares their story through writing. I find that to be true. While composing my story, I had a realization that brought me to tears.

I had thought I slid into depression because I was working a job that was not emotionally fulfilling. I was wrong. It began when I abandoned myself at nine years old by adopting the name Brittany. At such a tender age, I had no idea the pain it would later cause me. What felt like a solution at the time, was something insidious and ate away at my soul until I had almost nothing left. However, if I had to do it all over again, I wouldn't change a thing. My experiences allowed me to deeply appreciate being me.

Thank you for taking the time to read my story. I'm grateful and I appreciate you.

ABOUT THE AUTHOR

MIAUWLING OEI

Miauwling Oei is an Alignment Coach and helps people align with their next right action. Her mission and greatest passion are to provide people with simple tools to help them get through incredibly difficult moments in life. She was seconds away from taking her own life on January 13, 2012 when she felt the deepest love that rocked her to the core. To this day, it was the greatest miracle she has ever experienced and thus her journey within began.

Her work is an integration of her studies and practices to further embody herself and span across Kundalini yoga, Katonah yoga, gratitude journaling, Reiki, the law of attraction and S Factor movement. She lives in New York with her cat Amber. In her spare time, she loves to dance and take long walks in nature.

linktr.ee/miauwling
www.instagram.com/miauw_ling/

TRICIA MCKENNA

THE CREATION OF "A HEART GROUNDED"

*D*o you ever wonder where some of your thoughts and beliefs come from? Or, how your thoughts and beliefs impact your life as you know it? When we are born, we are vulnerable to those that are caring for us, and we trust them to take care of us, guide us and nurture us. Many children are born from lineages that are less than ideal, and yet they somehow find a way to live a thriving life. Those who have taken early childhood struggles and turned them into blessings have always inspired me.

This is the notion that inspired me to share my story. My journey is one of a hardscrabble life and heart-fought victories. All my challenges have opened up new insights and spiritual paths that led me to a life I am learning to love and lessons I want to share with others. I've battled back from alcohol and drug use, family neglect and abuse, and childhood health problems. I'm a mom, a veteran Real Estate Broker, Kundalini yoga teacher, and the creator of the *"A Heart Grounded"* movement. My passion is helping uplift others to find their own light, by helping them develop their own spiritual practice, and allowing them to experience healing, prosperity, and joy in their homes and personal lives.

I was born in the cool fall month of October in Western New York. On the first day of my life, my precious physical body was fighting to be healthy, whole, and complete. I know now, what was making me ill is known as the herpes zoster virus and some babies never survive the birth process. This means that I have a compromised immune system and can be overly tired and sick a lot. I am so grateful God did not give up on me after I was born and continued to guide me on my path, no matter how many times I tried to take an exit.

A few years back a letter was found, written by my oldest, to my mom and I from that time while we stayed in the hospital after I was born, in which she shared her desire to have us both home because we were gone longer than planned when mom gave birth to me. Reading it now, as an adult, it reminds me of how hard it was to be any of us at the time. All of us were fighting for survival in our own ways.

CHALLENGES AND BLESSINGS

Growing up, I was the youngest of three girls. When I was just one year old, my mom decided for good to live a life apart from our father.

Dad was a Vietnam Veteran who had PTSD and suffered from side effects from Agent Orange. He was absent for most of my early childhood due to excessive drug and alcohol use. When I was nine, my dad became sober enough to be a part of our lives and I was able to visit him on the weekends. My dad tried really hard to be there for me once he was sober. He would talk about his conversations with God and how God saved him after he suffered a stroke and a heart attack. My dad was born on Christmas Day, and he was the seventh son born into his family. Dad felt this made his relationship with God special, even at times I heard him talking about being the son of God. He told me that when you have a relationship with God you are never alone. He loved God with all his heart and often in his struggles would cry out to God.

Knowing what I know now, I know my mom was doing the best she could when she made the tough decision to leave our home with my sisters and me. She thought that leaving him was what was best for us, because he was deep in his mental health recovery from PTSD and alcohol abuse at that time.

For me, my poor health continued through my adolescent years. It often included missing school and extracurricular activities, and frequent visits to the doctor for testing and allergy shots. My mom tried to keep me active, and even placed me in an indoor soccer league one winter. During this time, I was very close with my oldest sister and kept close to her. I remember struggling to keep up with schoolwork, with grades that barely allowed me to move to the next grade level.

When I was eleven years old, I experienced a long cold and flu season. I became sicker than normal and was having several issues with my left eye. There was an eighteen-month span when I was homeschooled and in and out of the hospital while they figured out what was happening with me. My dad's brother would come and pray over me and share the word of God with me. After several hospital stays and many laser surgeries, I had my left eye surgically removed the summer between seventh and eighth grade. Being surrounded by so much uncertainty, what I actually remember most was being so angry that my eye socket would not be ready for a prosthetic eye in time for an eighth-grade dance I had been invited to, and I would still be wearing an eye patch. I hated that I had to wear an eye patch. Everything about it was terrible: the tape made me break out, my eyelashes would get all gooey and my eye socket itched a lot. The impact of losing my eye truly took a toll on my sense of self-worth and confidence. Still today I often struggle to enjoy getting pictures taken, am very uncomfortable on video, and often bump into people when in crowded areas because of the lack of peripheral vision. Funnily enough, people often ask me if I can see out of my artificial eye!

WILD CHILD

After my eye was removed I returned to school in time for ninth grade and entered high school. I had my first alcoholic drink when I was thirteen years old. I remember the day clearly. The Buffalo Bills were playing the Miami Dolphins in the AFC Championship Game. I was hanging out with a bunch of older teenagers my sister had over. They thought I was super cool because I was able to shotgun a beer on my first attempt.

My drinking subsided a bit when my first nephew was born. I was blessed to be the one entrusted with his care on the weekends while my sister and her husband worked weekend jobs to make ends meet. I would go to school from Monday to- Friday, and on Friday evening my sister would pick me up to stay at her apartment and babysit. When I was 14, they moved away to Arizona, and I became the only child left at home. I filled my time with chasing boys, drinking, and acting wild. At fifteen, I tried other drugs. One summer night when I was out with a girlfriend chasing boys, I crashed my dad's brand-new Geo Tracker on our way home. We were trying to put the convertible top down while driving and ended up in the ditch. We were both in rough shape from the crash, and it would not be the only one of my dad's vehicles that I would crash during this period of my life. By God's grace, I graduated high school in Angola, New York.

After graduation, I met my sons' father. Two months later, at seventeen years old, I found myself pregnant. In May of 1998, my first son was born. Six weeks after he was born, I found out his dad had been cheating on me throughout my entire pregnancy. I was in shock when I heard from the other girl. At this time, my mom and my sisters had already all left New York and moved to Arizona. With no immediate family, I was determined to get out of New York, and decided to pack up what I could and fly with my two-month-old son to Arizona to be around a family who could help me. A few months later, my son's father followed me there. I held onto hope that it was a sign he was changing; that things would be different. When my first son was 9 months old, I found out I was pregnant once again. At that time, I found a way for us to get our own studio apartment in Mesa. I was working as a waitress and taking full time 18 credit hours at a community college. My sons' father was a stay at home parent. One night when I returned home after work, our neighbor's boyfriend came pounding on our apartment door, looking for my sons' father. He was screaming at him about being at a party at the girlfriend's home and accusing him of some terrible things. Shortly after that, my sons' father was on a Greyhound bus back to New York never to return to Arizona. My second son was born that December.

For six years, I raised my two boys on my own again by God's grace, without a penny from their father. For the first few years on my own with my boys, I was able to remain sober. Really, it was because I had no time for anything else. As my boys got a little older and started elementary school, I became more comfortable leaving them with sitters so I could go out with my roommates. In one home we lived in, I had two other single moms living with us, so we would pool our money to hire a sitter so the three of us could go out for ladies' night which usually consisted of drinking. For a few months, I even found myself working at a club to make ends meet.

NEW CHAPTERS AND LESSONS

In 2005, I met my now-husband, at a job one of my ex-boyfriends had helped me find. God can be funny like that. My husband inspired me to get into Real Estate. He happened to have two sons like me, so we wanted to have some flexibility for someone to be at home when our four boys came home from school. We had worked together for over a year before we started dating. What first started out as a friendship turned into us moving in together. My youngest son was struggling at this time. He struggled to keep up in school and was getting in trouble at home. I was doing a lot of research on how to help him when a friend invited me to a seminar at the University of Phoenix. That is where I first learned that a child's health and brain function can be affected by the state of the mother's womb as early as six months preconception!

I was absolutely mind blown by what I learned at the seminar. I had gone into it to find information to help my son, but instead I found the information God wanted me to find to help me heal myself. After the convention, I started to investigate what my mom's life was like six months before I was conceived, and became curious as to what thought patterns and energies I was exposed to in utero that would have contributed to my health and life experiences.

A few years later, my sons started to transition to living out of our home. My eldest got a football scholarship and moved to South Dakota, while my youngest left and moved in with my sister. Suddenly, I found myself living without the two boys that I had been in charge of for over half of my life! Nobody prepared me for having my kids' transition out of the home. My life as I had known it to be felt like it was falling apart. I felt completely out of control. For weeks after dropping my son off at college, I was super depressed, I would go into his old room and cry for hours on end, and constantly check in on him at college, a habit he was super annoyed about. My husband was confused by my behavior, because he saw this as a time of celebration for our son, as well as us, as we enter the empty nester season. As far as he saw it, everything was going well, and I wanted to see it that way too.

Having the boys out of the home allowed my husband 1 and I to spend more time together. I started to get us to try new things like painting together in order to build our connection. One of my very first paintings was a heart with roots. I shared this painting in one of my women's groups. They said it looked like something that belonged on the cover of a book. I named the painting *A Heart Grounded*.

BECOMING *A HEART GROUNDED*

In December 2018, I got a strong conviction from the Holy Spirit to stop drinking. On a Monday morning in January 2019, I went to a 12-step meeting after another weekend of stressing out about how my sons and husband were living their lives, and experiencing the overwhelming feeling that things were not going as planned. I was living my days worrying and stressing about everyone except myself. This caused me to be distracted throughout my workday and I felt physically exhausted. It was terrible enough for me to seek relief from my emotional pain by going to a meeting that morning.

I remember the day so clearly. I was at work, and most of my thoughts were so focused on everything that was going wrong in my life that I decided to just surrender to God and ask him to show me what I can do right now to stop the suffering I was experiencing. It was at that moment I heard a message to "look for a 12-step meeting near you" It was around 10:45am when I did a Google search and I found out that there was a meeting starting a half-mile from my office at 12 noon.

I stepped into the room and heard what I needed to hear. I immediately asked one of the ladies who had shared her story that day if she would sponsor me. I was ready to do whatever it took to get myself out of this dark place.

She graciously accepted but took a few days to reach out to me when she told me she would call me that night. I can laugh now, sharing this, but back then I felt rejected when I did not hear from her right away. All my feelings went into overdrive all over again. She finally reached out a couple of days later and apologized for taking so long. She explained what had been going on and then offered to help with what came next. We got along well as we were both married with teenage children.

I immediately started working on the 12 Steps. The first two steps were rather easy for me, because I already believed in God thanks to my dad and uncle. I even believed it was my faith in God that had gotten me through my life until then. But things became uncomfortable when my sponsor had me start working on step four, which is "making a searching and fearless moral inventory of ourselves". This is where the real work started; this is where I pulled out all the choices I had made up to this point. My sponsor had me start journaling all the memories I had, all the way from my first memory to the current day. I found this very challenging. I had very few memories to share prior to the medical trauma I experienced as a young girl. This remains the most uncomfortable part of my spiritual practice.

STEP 11

In July 2019, I started working on step 11 of the 12 steps which reads "sought through prayer and meditation to improve our conscious contact with God as we understand him, praying only for knowledge of his will for us and the power to carry it out". My meditation practice came to me in the form of a 10-week Kundalini yoga/meditation program, based on the 10 energetic bodies. When the program started, I was the first participant to complete the 40-

day 22-minute meditation challenge. I was able to keep up with it because I felt different after the first few attempts and *wanted* to continue. In January 2020, I received my one-year chip in the 12-step program.

Because of my reliance on God, I have been able to persevere through the hardest of times. It has helped me develop a daily discipline in the form of a non-negotiable daily spiritual practice. Since establishing that, I have been able to stop drinking, lose 30lbs, heal my relationships, grow a prosperous business, including earning a YPN Top 40 under 40 award, helping my adult children financially transition to adulthood. Slowly but surely, my thoughts of being broken, not being enough, and worst-case scenarios happening to my family members are all being rewired, and my path is being redirected to be *"A Heart Grounded"*.

Today, my daily spirituality consists of waking up before sunrise to have alone time with God every single day. Upon waking, I do the wake-up set in bed and thank God when I put my feet on the ground. After that, I drink 32oz of warm water with either lemon or lime. Then I move outside or to my mediation space for my time alone with God. That is when I practice Kundalini yoga and do a 11 minute meditation before starting the rest of my day. I also have a meditation/prayer practice I do before bed. It is said in Kundalini yoga that when we heal, we can heal seven generations in both directions. For me, Kundalini yoga is the fastest way I can enter a state of peace and joy.

I am forever grateful for the multiple people throughout my life that talked about God and shared their faith with me. I now see certain milestones in my life, where God took me out of a bad situation and redirected me to the people he placed in my life!

Helping others to go within and to learn more about themselves, to develop their own spiritual practice so they too can learn to be "*A Heart Grounded*" remains a true passion of mine. No matter where you go, no matter what you do, no matter who you're with, the one contributing factor in all circumstances is you! You are with you from the time you come out of the womb until the time you die. You will spend the most amount of time with yourself, so why not get to know yourself better? Taking time every day to get to know yourself, work on yourself, forgive yourself, and offer your self-compassion is one of the most transformational things that you can do in this life form.

ABOUT THE AUTHOR

TRICIA MCKENNA

Tricia McKenna is the creator of "A Heart Grounded" movement and offers mentoring services as well as heart-centered real estate services. In 2014, Tricia was a recipient of the Top 40 under 40 Award from the Young Professional Network for Realtors. Committed to a daily spiritual practice, she has transformed her early childhood health problems, family trauma, and addictions. Driven by her own journey, Tricia is focused on empowering others to achieve their dreams, get unstuck, break destructive habits and patterns in their lives so that they can experience freedom, self-expression, joy, and abundance. Whether it's personal, business, or financial aspects of your life, Tricia incorporates birth charts, Kundalini yogic science, mediation, and energetic practices to help you achieve your dreams.

Tricia currently resides in Arizona with her husband, Paul and her dog, Rhea. She is a proud mom, wife, daughter, sister, and entrepreneur.

www.aheartgrounded.com
www.instagram.com/aheartgrounded/

17

ULRIKE ZIMMERMANN

GIRL IN THE MIRROR

I was born into a family where matriarchy has ruled for generations. My mother is a strong character, my grandmother even stronger, and from stories I've heard, my great-grandmother used to be the strongest of them all as she raised 5 children all by herself at the time of reconstruction after the Nazi regime had fallen.

My biological father hasn't played much of a role in my life—at least not physically. In hindsight though, I realise that I've always felt the need to overcompensate for his absence, or rather the absence of a strong masculine energy in my life, even though from a very young age, my stepdad has accompanied me in life. He's a very sensitive, kind and gentle soul, which nowadays I see as his most auspicious qualities, but back in the days of puberty and young adulthood I used to despise him for his softness.

4 Y/O

Love is my natural state. It's the only thing I've ever experienced. My parents love me with all their heart and it makes me feel safe to express myself and explore my environment.

I love weekends at my grandparents. This means fun, playtime and hot chocolate. Today my granny is in a really good mood, so she allows me to take her dresses and high-heels (stuffed with a bunch of socks) and even put on some of her rouge and lipstick. I put on my favorite soundtrack from the spice girls and there we go. The stage is mine. Three minutes of dancing, singing and performing for my audience, which consists of my grandma, grandad and some stuffed animals.

5 Y/O

It's my birthday and I was given the best present ever: a doll that makes sounds when you hug her. I call her Wendy. Wendy is my most favorite doll in the world now and I will take her with me everywhere.

I love sitting next to my grandpa in the car, because he always listens to good music. We are singing a duet. Something from Elton John with a crocodile.

My parents, me and Wendy are in a pizzeria and next to our table there is this sad looking girl. Her hair is uncombed, her teeth are black and she has no toys for herself. I ask my mom why she looks so strange and smells so bad and my mom tells me that not every child has parents like I do who take good care of them. It makes me sad and I suddenly can't go on with life like I used to. I have to do something to make this girl feel better. I look at Wendy and that's it. If Wendy makes me feel so good, maybe it will make this girl feel good too. I say goodbye to Wendy and give her to the girl.

6 Y/O

School is hard. I am going to an elementary school with a focus on musical education, because my family wanted to support my love of performance. In class my teacher makes us sing aloud. She doesn't like my voice—she thinks it sounds crooked. Everyone is laughing. My teacher only likes 'the good ones', and I ain't one of them.

My classmates don't like me either. They don't want to play with me or have me on their dodgeball team or invite me over after school. I don't really get it. I just want to belong. This is something I have never experienced before. It feels shameful and makes me uneasy.

7 Y/O

There's a violin concert in school today for some of my classmates to perform. They have friends and our teacher approves of them, so I guess I should start playing the violin too. Yes, I will definitely start playing the violin.

My parents think I am joking, so I would have to pay for myself to get my first violin. And I do.

I really love this instrument and I am also surprisingly good at it. I am actually way better than the others. My teacher loves me now. I am her number one. Ulli here, Ulli there. Ulli plays the first violin everywhere. Now the others should like me, right? Because I am now good, really good, at something. But they don't. It feels even more off. I am walking on eggshells. They detest me, they make fun of me, they exclude me. I barely exist to them.

I don't know how to handle all the negativity from my classmates, so I just shut up and hold myself back. I try not to attract attention, so they can forget about me. Sometimes this works, but sometimes it doesn't. Distancing myself from everyone—including myself—seems a price worth paying to not be made fun of.

9 Y/O

There is one girl who especially hates me more than the others. She seems to be the leader in our class. Those she approves of, everyone likes. Those she doesn't find worthy, nobody likes. It rained yesterday and there are still puddles everywhere on the playground. I walk through one. The girl sees me and starts screaming and shaming me: "The puddles are filled with Ulli's piss, because that's the only thing she does." Everyone laughed. I didn't.

Today there's a letter in our mailbox. It says, "Give us money or you will be hurt." I am paralyzed and filled with pure panic. Why is this happening to me? What is wrong with me?

After the weekend, they say the letter with the threat was just a joke. "Don't be such a party pooper. No wonder nobody likes you!"

My nervous system shuts down. I can't sleep and most definitely can't go back to school, because school wants to eat me alive in my dreams. School has arms and legs and a really, really nasty laugh. And it wants to eat me.

10 Y/O

It's the week of our musical. I am playing the tourist guide and also the first violin. I love the attention. I love the performance. This is where I feel safe. Safe to be and express myself. This is probably the best week of elementary school.

13 Y/O

Over the summer holidays, puberty got to me. I change my multi-colored hairdo to a walnut brown bob, my clothes show off the first signs of tiny breasts and I know how to use just enough make-up to look more mature. Not my granny's make-up but my own. People seem to perceive me differently. My classmates look at me differently - especially the boys. Somehow over the past ten weeks, life has taken a 180 degree turn. No nasty comments, no disgusted looks. Instead I am invited to sleepovers and get-togethers. I don't really get it. Am I famous now?

I am so used to being the outsider, the loser, the weird girl, that I have no idea how to handle this new situation. I don't know what to feel, how to behave or what to expect. I am so overwhelmed and afraid to lose this position again that I feel more uneasy than ever. I must make sure to never go back to where I've been. I must stay popular. I need to demonstrate my new power.

If that means becoming like them, so be it. What do I care if others feel bullied or shamed by me? I can't handle their weakness anyway. Aren't I doing them a favor by showing them their place?

16 Y/O

My parents are a pain in the arse. They call me coldhearted and express how hurt and disappointed they are. This should hurt me, but I don't feel anything. Not a single emotion. I haven't for years to be honest. I am chasing after adventures, boys and excitement to make me feel something, anything. I don't know how to get rid of the numbness and loneliness, because even though on the outside I seem to be happy, always being surrounded by friends, I feel like I have no idea who this person is that I see in the mirror when I brush my teeth.

The years go by, and so do the party nights and boys. Every month there is another crush. Everytime they fall for me, I run from them. Every weekend another boytoy, more alcohol, cigarettes and wild nights. But still, inside of me, there is only this bottomless ocean of emptiness that I don't know how to fill.

17 Y/O

My mom is sick. She isn't able to take part in family life as she used to. She is so burned out at work that she has no energy left—not even to keep crying most days. She freaking scares the sh*t out of me, but I only blame and shame her for her weakness. I know this is wrong. I know I should be there for her, but I'm captivated by my own inability to feel and express my emotions.

If there are two things I can't handle, they're emotions and weakness—and she throws both in my face.

My parents and I are in a very lonely episode. My mom occupies the bedroom, my dad pretends to do stuff outside, and my door is always closed.

We rarely speak, and if we do, we fight.

On our dinner table there is always one big chair for the huge pink elephant in the room, the one that nobody wants to talk about. Because if we do, it means we need to talk about it all.

18 Y/O

It's the day of my 18th birthday. I have been out partying all night and stayed at a friend's house. My mom is in therapy on the other side of Austria and my dad is home by himself and our four cats. He reads the paper while caressing one of the cats in his lap.

He hears a knock on the door. My dad gets up, wondering who it might be. He looks out of the window and sees a man with a huge bundle of white roses. He thinks my granny sent over flowers for my birthday and opens the door.

The man on the other side of the door sill looks befuddled.

My dad asks how he can help and the man answers: "I am here for my daughter. It's her birthday today. She's turning 18. I wanted to give her some flowers."

Now my dad is the one looking befuddled. The man on the other side is my biological father.

19 Y/O

Finally it's graduation day. I am beyond excited to move to the big city. Vienna is where I'm supposed to be. I am made for the city. I am made for glamour, nightly parties, fancy food and international acquaintances. I can't wait to move and study there. I will study something nobody expects from me: water science and technology. I will prove everybody wrong who ever disrespected me. I will show them who the boss is.

20 Y/O

It is very different from what I expected studying to be. Everyday I'm hustling, but I know I still need to prove myself. I just need to try harder to do it. I am not stupid, I can't be stupid. I must succeed. Even if this means getting up at 6am every day, going to campus until the evening and spending my nights on my desk, deeply wrapped up in my studies.

I don't know why my body does this to me. Chronic tonsillitis. As if I didn't already have enough on my agenda! But I mean, there's a pill for everything. Vitamins in the morning, antibiotics for lunch, and some painkillers with an aperitivo. The pills keep me going.

The doctor doesn't want to prescribe me any more pills and wants me to rest instead, but I can't slow down. I am not a failure. I can't fail. I refuse to.

Something is wrong. Something is very wrong. Is this a dream? Am I asleep? Because I can't move and I can't open my eyes. I breathe, so I must be alive. My face is swollen, I can feel that, but the rest of my body feels motionless. What the hell is going on with me? I am lying alone in bed, unable to get myself a glass of water or go to the toilet. The anxiety is creeping in. It runs me over like a tsunami, accompanied by its friends: trauma, grief and deep sadness. I have nowhere to escape to. I can't run away and I can't distract myself, so there is no option but to surrender.

Forced by my paralyzed body, I have no choice but to look my suppressed emotions straight in the eye—raw , real, pure and in their full power.

They are filling my emptiness, escaping from the darkest corners of my subconscious into the open. And for the first time in a decade, I can cry. In fact, I am not able to stop crying. I allow myself to fully feel and own my pain. The spell is broken.

21 Y/O

I don't know how I made this man my boyfriend. He is much older, knows what he wants in life and owns a company with employees. I have no idea why he wants to be with me. I have nothing to offer, so I need to try really hard to keep him. I am around, whenever he needs me. I am becoming his dream girl. I will be the perfect lawyer for him, since water science didn't work out. I will be the perfect housewife to him too—I will even give him children. For him I will stay in this city that makes me feel so disconnected, because I would do anything for him. I think this is love, right?

22 Y/O

He was my first love and now he is gone. He said I keep him from being happy, but didn't I do it all? Didn't I do everything for him to approve of me? Didn't I even give up my own dreams to become who he wanted me to be?

23 Y/O

This law degree pisses me off. I don't like getting paid to help people fight. I don't like sitting in front of a desk. I like travelling. I like yoga. I like foreign cultures. And I like this girl. I have never been with a girl before, but she is different and she makes me feel different. She sees me beyond my flaws. Nobody has ever touched me the way she touches me, because she not only touches my skin, but my soul. She has the ability to see me, my truth and to hold me accountable to that. She makes me a better person. And I take care of her, because she has this thing with anxiety and depression. From this day on, she doesn't need to worry anymore, because I am now here for her. I will take over whatever she can't take on.

Finally I have the courage to stop this farce. To quit law school and get my life together. To move away from this awful city and closer to Pacha Mama. I thank God for this woman, who allows me to see my path clearly and where it leads. I will be moving in with her soon, and it will be amazing. I will help her become healthy and she will help me find my purpose.

I am beyond excited. I just booked my first yoga teacher training in Guatemala. Three months of self exploration. But what will my girlfriend do without me?

She sits me down and tells me it's not working. She wants to end it, because with me by her side, she simply can't get healthy and will forever be trapped. I am speechless. I am broken. Why is it always the same? I give my all and my partners say it is not enough. I am not enough.

With a broken heart and no place to call home, but all the courage I could find inside of me, I took off to Guatemala. The yoga teacher training is amazing. Guatemala is amazing. Travelling with and by myself is lifting the veil of my negative self-perception. I can witness my own inner beauty for the first time in my life.

24 Y/O

Here I am again. In the middle of Asia. Six months by myself, after I fell for another toxic relationship with someone who stole from me and abused me.

Another journey deeper within. But this time, I am finally able to hold myself accountable for all that has happened. I am prepared to declare full responsibility for the contributions I made to my experiences in life, instead of shaming and blaming others. Enough of that. It is time to grow up.

25 Y/O

It is freaking painful to go deep, to bluntly see and own my unhealed parts. Growth hurts. I want to give up so badly, because I am now starting to see what my contribution was to all the experiences I made in life. It was never about the others! It was always about me. Now I can't return to the safety of shaming my ex partners, the mean girls in school or the bullying teachers. But the hardest part is forgiving myself for all the ways I hurt myself and sabotaged my happiness.

Even though the pain is overwhelming, I can also already feel how my life is shifting. It becomes a life where I am no longer a victim of my circumstances, but where I am in charge of it. I can see and sense the woman I am becoming, and I can't wait to meet her.

26 Y/O

With every day that passes, I am stepping more into my power. I know my worth and I am not settling for less. All the radical self love and accountability from the past years has led to a life that fulfills me deeply.

My coaching business and yoga teacher trainings are flourishing. It is so easy and satisfying to work with my clients.

The relationship with my partner is rooted in trust, respect and fun and I feel at home being with him.

I feel an ease and lightness to life, like a daily trip to the playground.

27 Y/O

When I look in the mirror now, I see a woman that amazes me. She is fierce, passionate, soft and gentle at once.

When I look in the mirror now, I see all the struggles she has overcome in her life already and how she owns every bit of her story with so much grace.

When I look in the mirror now, I see everyone that has added to the experiences this woman has absorbed so far.

When I look in the mirror now, I already see the auspicious woman I am yet to become.

ABOUT THE AUTHOR

ULRIKE ZIMMERMANN

Ulrike Zimmermann is the founder of Tantra Yoga Austria.

Driven by her own journey to her authentic, powerful self, Ulrike has gathered tools and techniques from all over the world to heal deep, ancestral wounds and beliefs and now shares her gift with the world.

With her holistic approach to coaching, she helps people to heal their trauma, step into their power and become leaders in their field. Through the combination of tantric practices, coaching tools and healing exercises, she offers her clients a variety of possibilities to achieve their soul mission.

Over the past few years, Ulrike has specialized in working with cyclical-based business, which makes her a pioneer in the field of female leadership.

www.tantrayoga-austria.com
www.instagram.com/tantrayoga_austria/

ABOUT THE PUBLISHER
BRIDGET AILEEN SICSKO

WEBSITE   PODCAST

Bridget Aileen Sicsko is the founder of Exalted Publishing House, a podcast host and a visibility coach. She helps successful entrepreneurs stand out and be featured as leaders in their industry by sharing powerful stories, writing best-selling books and gaining global recognition. Bridget believes in the power of words, stories and voices to shift our view of reality, our potential and our purpose on the planet. In addition, she considers herself a master community builder and has gathered hundreds of female leaders in her online community, mastermind program, networking events, and women's circles. Bridget also hosts a podcast, The Gathering MVMT, where she has interviewed over 75 entrepreneurs, TEDx speakers, authors, thought-leaders, and visionaries to discuss success consciousness, leadership, kundalini yoga, energetics, and quantum reality. Bridget has been featured in Authority Magazine, Women's Business Daily, Thrive Global, The Medium, on Ticker News, News 12 New York and several podcasts. She lives in New Jersey with her husband and her border collie beagle, Finn.

www.bridgetaileen.com

www.instagram.com/blissfulbridget

18

ABOUT EXALTED PUBLISHING HOUSE

*E*xalted Publishing House produces books that move hearts and minds.

We are an *indie-book publisher + visibility accelerator* for leaders, CEOS, entrepreneurs and business owners who want to get more eyes on their story.

Exalted Publishing House has a simple philosophy: change the world through words. Our aim is to work with a small number of entrepreneurs, organizations and businesses each year to uphold the highest standard of intimacy and personalization in the cathartic writing and publishing process. We mainly work in the realms of the alternative, disenfranchised & different by sharing stories that aren't always spoken through mainstream channels.

CORPORATE BOOKS

We create multi-author books for business owners, CEOS and organizations to highlight the stories of their mission, brand, teams and employees.

MULTI-AUTHOR BOOKS & VISIBILITY PROJECTS

We work with leaders and entrepreneurs who want to get featured in top tier publications and podcasts and share their story to elevate their brand.

If you would like to purchase a 100+ bulk order of any of our books for schools, organizations, teams, book clubs at a discounted rate, please contact bridget@bridgetaileen.com for details and prices.

OTHERS BOOKS BY EXALTED PUBLISHING HOUSE

Legacy Speaks, Powerhouse Women Leading Lives Worth Remembering

Success Codes, Secrets To Success You Weren't Taught In School

Lineage Speaks, Women Who Carry The Torch For Future Generations

Coming Soon...

"Where Social Work Can Lead You"

FURTHER ASSISTANCE

If you or someone you know is struggling or needs help, please know you are not alone and seek the help you need.

Suicide Prevention Hotline:

United States: 1-800-273-8255

Better Help: https://www.betterhelp.com/

Made in the USA
Las Vegas, NV
23 January 2022

42181017R00118